OCCULT IN ART

THE OCCULT IN ART

THE
OCCULT
IN ART

Fred Gettings

RIZZOLI
NEW YORK

A Studio Vista book first published in Great Britain
by Cassell Ltd.

Published in the United States of America in 1979 by:

Rizzoli INTERNATIONAL PUBLICATIONS, INC.
712 Fifth Avenue/New York 10019

Library of Congress Catalog Card Number: 78-57910
ISBN: 0-8478-0190-X

Designed by Fred Gettings
Filmset and printed in Great Britain by
BAS Printers Limited, Over Wallop, Hampshire

CONTENTS

INTRODUCTION

The Questing Eye

OCCULTISM IS THE study of the spiritual world which is hidden from ordinary vision. The word itself is derived from the latin *occulta*, 'hidden things', and implies that the visible world is not the only one of importance to man. According to occult teaching, a rich spiritual world lies all around, and it is only through a study of this world that man may fully explain his position in the cosmos, and come to some real understanding of himself. This is the underlying message in such illustrations as the engraving from Robert Fludd[1] (figure 1) which portrays man's soul, his feminine *anima*, standing in the womb of the macrocosm, of which even the zodiac is merely a part. Such an illustration proclaims the fundamental law of occultism which is expressed in the tradition that God made two things in his own image—the Cosmos and Man—a tradition expressed in the hermetic dictum, *As Above, so Below*.[2]

This invisible soul world is also the true domain of art. 'Where the spirit does not work with the hand, there is no art', said Leonardo da Vinci[3] briefly, and five hundred years later, when he felt constrained to speak of the spiritual in art, Kandinsky[4] wrote, 'The work of art is born of the artist in a mysterious and secret way', for he saw the artist as a magician bringing art into materialisation from the invisible realms of spirit.

The true artist speaks the language of the soul, and those who wish to approach art must learn to some extent this language. There is, however, a class of art which speaks a particularly sophisticated language, for it seeks to encapsulate a secret symbolism of forms and structures which are intended to be understood only by the initiated, or by those who have in one way or another developed the sensitivity of the soul to occult truths. This is the hidden art, which speaks a very special language of the spirit. It was this secret art which the thirteenth century mystic Hildegard of Bingen had in mind when, anxious that the

1. Engraving by de Vries from Robert Fludd's *Utriusque cosmi. . . historia,* 1621.

2. Marble floor zodiac, dated 1207, in the nave of San Miniato al Monte, Florence.

2

occult illustrations to her visionary book should be approached in the right way, she pleaded with her reader,

> But you who look upon this picture, understand that it also has a meaning for the inner soul.[5]

This plea is absolute for all time, and in a sense applies to all art, but it is especially relevant to those works which have consciously been produced in order to express occult ideas in a secret way.

This book is a sort of extensive footnote to Hildegard's request, for it intends to introduce the reader to something of the nature of the hidden art which speaks to the soul. It has been written to encourage a growth of awareness of the extent to which artists have striven to express in hidden forms the inner world of soul—the *anima mundi* of Hildegard, the *spirito* of Leonardo, the *innerer Klang* of Kandinsky—by revealing a number of the devices by which such artists have attempted to create an exclusive art which speaks in parables to the initiated, and remains a hidden art for those who do not understand.

The abandon with which I leap in quotation from Hildegard to Leonardo, and then to Kandinsky, indicates that I have not in any way attempted to trace the historical development of the secret art: this would take a knowledge, if not a lifespan, way beyond my own expectations. My aim has been rather to examine in some depths a few of the occult strains within works of art which are more or less familiar to the informed public, and to show how such works, unless viewed within their occult contexts, almost totally evade real appreciation. This aim has to some extent been achieved by calling into question certain presuppositions about works of art, and by showing that the established art-historical approach is not always the correct one.

In the first chapters I have attempted to show how certain strains in mediaeval art—particularly in ecclesiastical architecture—cannot be fully appreciated without a living knowledge of the astrological concepts which permeated mediaeval life. I have taken for granted the fact that every element in the design of churches and cathedrals was intended to be meaningful, and generally expressive of a hidden knowledge, for those capable of reading these forms. One of the important presumptions of the non-specialist historian which has been called into question is that concerning the orientation of churches, for it is generally supposed that churches were built 'towards the east'—hence the common term *east end* for the head of the church. In fact, as this chapter indicates, the orientation is

3. Mosaic of Christ enthroned, in apse of San Miniato al Monte, Florence, *c.* 1297. (See colour plate 53)

3

not always towards the east, and indeed very frequently an ecclesiastical building has been sited in order to express some mystery in relation to occult or heretical strains within its architectural design. Thus, the orientation of the basilica of San Miniato al Monte is related to the minutiae of marble decoration, to the floor zodiac (figure 2), and to the vast apse mosaic (figure 3). Such an orientation, and the themal links between these decorative motives, would not make sense in terms of ordinary art-historical presumptions, but make perfect sense when related to the occult astrological tradition.

I have dealt in some depth with the fascinating heresy of the two Jesus children, not merely because this is still largely an unexplored occult theme important in the development of hidden art, and not even because it links so profoundly with astrological imagery, but mainly because I feel that the seminal work of Steiner[6] in this field has not yet received the attention it deserves, and many of his ideas are of immediate and profound relevance to the understanding not only of occult art, but of the modern predicament of art. The approach to this heresy—for it is undoubtedly a heresy nowadays, even though it was originally rooted in early Christian esotericism—calls into question very many art-historical prejudices, simply because the idea of this heresy has not yet been accommodated into the approach to art history. In many cases, therefore, our appreciation of this heresy depends upon our looking at the old images in a new light. For example, the 'dual' images of single works which depict the Jesus of the Magi, and the Jesus of the Shepherds together (figure 5), and which would be explained by art historians in terms of 'continuous representation', must be seen in an entirely new way if the heretical aspect of such works is to be grasped. The very novelty of this new approach to the old images and heresies has already had a deleterious effect, so that there has been a tendency to link some images which were never intended to illustrate the heresy with the heresy itself. For example, the woodcut at figure 4 has been linked by one historian[7] with the two Jesus children imagery, but in fact it belongs to a tradition which began humbly enough as an illustration to a story told by Albertus Magnus,[8] having nothing whatsoever to do with religion, let alone with the heresy.

Within the space available, I have been unable to do more than dabble in the occult strains within the Renaissance—this is fortunately one of the few areas of occultism which has received attention from art historians

4. Woodcut from F. de Retza, *Historia beata Mariae Virginis,* 1471.

5. Sixth century ivory relief, perhaps Coptic: Adoration of the Magi, and Nativity scene from the apocryphal *Protevangelium*. British Museum, London. (See colour plate 54)

Si tactuf mox natū feras apperire valet. Cur mater verbi natū virgo non generaret. Alb° de motibꝰ aīaliuꝳ pte fcd̄a trac. 1.°

4

5

6. Sandro Botticelli, *Primavera, c.*1478.
Uffizi, Florence.

7. Leonardo da Vinci, *Virgin Mary and Child,
with Saint Anne and Saint John, c.* 1505.
National Gallery, London.

6

7

in recent times, and so the chapter on what I call the *Mercury of Angels* is intended merely to complement or extend work already done. The various art-historical prejudices challenged in this chapter are deeply rooted, and may best be indicated in an innocent-sounding question about Botticelli's most famous picture, the *Primavera* (figure 6). What is it that permits a painting of a largely unknown subject, garnished with an imaginative title which the artist himself would not recognize, already in a faded state so far as the pigment is concerned, overtly concerned with neo-Platonic conceits which virtually lapsed into obscurity during the Renaissance and which are now understood by a mere handful of scholars, a picture furthermore which is badly displayed in the gallery, and by virtue of its fame generally inaccessible to the public as an object of quiet contemplation—what is it that has made this picture one of the most famous in the world? My answer to this question would challenge the stock presumptions of most art historians, for it would point to my belief that what is great about this picture is precisely what is hidden. It is no element with which the conscious mind might wrestle, but the secret geometry and symbolism, the hidden qualities, which pull one towards this image, and make one's soul admit its greatness. The same might be said—and has been said— about the presently world-famous Leonardo cartoon (figure 7), which, I would maintain, deeply affects masses of people otherwise insensitive to more subtle aesthetic qualities, not because it is a great drawing (I personally do not think it is), but because of the secrets encapsulated in its *idea*, which speak directly to the soul. Art is frequently involved with the irrational elements in man, yet art history has generally presumed the rational to be supreme.

In my brief study of the fascinating heretical strains in late mediaeval art, which are so inextricably woven into the development and promulgation of occult ideas, I have chosen to treat of a little-known artist alongside one of the most famous painters of the sixteenth century—merging Bles with Bosch, so to speak—in order to indicate that a realistic approach to the hidden art must show no favours to the merely great. Much of the finest occult art has remained anonymous, and has flowed from the brushes of unknown painters. In regard to the prejudices of art history which one faces in the presence of these two artists there are magnificent extremes. On the one hand, since the work of Bles is largely ignored, and since his true intentions have remained obscured, his art has remained unexplored by art historians, who have on the whole concerned themselves with questions of provenance and influences: it is significant that the title accorded his roundel (figure 8) has been derived from a standard ecclesiastical tradition, whilst the picture is in fact heretical in intent. Bles' roundel is no more about 'The Fall' than Bosch's triptych is about 'Earthly Delights'. On the other hand, in the case of Bosch we find historians all too ready to link his imagery with occult and heretical concepts,[9] and the majority of historians are content to speak in general terms about his link with alchemical or Rosicrucian themes, or to explain away his imagery as the product of fantasy and demon-making (figure 9), the work of some isolated dream interpreter, dispensing a set of private images. This common prejudice ignores the historical fact that such an approach to art was simply not possible in late mediaeval Europe, and indeed has only become a common thing in relatively modern times. The windmill at which I tilt is the art-historical conceit that we know anything at all about Bosch, and that we may know anything about him without a profound understanding of the occult lore with which he himself was obviously very familiar.

The leap of a century from the different worlds of Bosch and Tintoretto to the private world of Blake is perhaps something of an optical illusion, for Blake is steeped in an occultism earlier than the late eighteenth century, depending as he does on the esoteric writings of Boehme, and the diagrams of Freher. Yet this leap significantly reflects the hiatus in the development of occult art which followed the profound shake-up of the Renaissance, as the leviathan occultism turned in its seabed. The collision which followed, in such externals as the Council of Trent, itself linked in some respects with the outer forms of the new, blinkered vision which pulled men's eyes down to the earth, in that necessary prelude to materialism, had the effect of completely changing not only art, but occultism. In spite of this, Blake must be recognised as an occultist, for he deals with visions of the spiritual world (figure 10)—yet he belongs to the nineteenth century not as an occultist, but as a romantic, and it is in this that his modern appeal may be understood. The truth is that it is the *romantic* approach to occultism—essentially sensation-seeking and therefore unhealthy—from which most people suffer today. In this fact we may find an understanding of Blake, for it is he, rather than the later occult painters such as Mondrian and Kandinsky,

8. Henri met de Bles, *The Fall, c.* 1530. Mauritshuis, The Hague. (See colour details at figures 96 and 97)

9. Detail f om Hieronymus Bosch, left-hand wing of *The Garden of Earthly Delights,* early 16th century. Prado, Madrid.

8

9

who expresses the modern crisis in art, which is of course a crisis of romanticism. The art-historical prejudice which one must challenge in the approach to Blake is endemic to the whole of art history, for few historians appear to be prepared to study occult ideas in depth, with the result that they fail to appreciate such men as Blake, whose very breath is coloured by Christian esotericism and Rosic-rucian lore.

Whilst I have glanced with regrettable brevity at Mondrian, Kandinsky and Ernst in two separate chapters, they should in fact be pulled together in unity, for each expresses in his own personal way the crisis in modern occultism. The first two fit very clearly into the modern stream of occultism by virtue of their contact with, and dependency upon, the modern schools originally vitalized by such occultists as Blavatsky and Steiner. The significant things about such artists, however, is that they represent a stream of personal occultism in art which is completely different from the universal, virtually anonymous occultism of the mediaeval art forms. They personalize occultism, yet at the same time they are identified with particular 'schools' of occultist persuasion. Ernst is not quite of this ilk: his work is almost a savage denial of both the universal anonymity of the ancient occultism, and the idea of occult schools themselves. The main trouble with the personal occultism at times evinced in the work of Ernst is that it may, when not exercised with infinite tact, and with considerable knowledge, merely degenerate into the charlatanism from which so much modern occultism suffers. The art-historical prejudice in regard to Mondrian, Kandinsky and Ernst is much the same as that we saw confronting the approach to Blake as an occultist—namely, an ignorance of the esoteric tradition, and a general refusal of historians to study the occult strains which have influenced these great artists. In fact, a serious study of the influence of the occult on Kandinsky (figure 11) has been initiated by such scholars as Ringbom,[10] but generally accounts of the antecedants of modern art are pathetically bereft of a real awareness of the contribution which nineteenth century occultism made to the formation of the modern attitude to art. My aim in this chapter, therefore, has been to set out a few lines of thought which might lead to a reassessment of the dependence of modern art on certain occult ideas. Unfortunately, for a really accurate picture of the development of modern art—especially of the so-called abstract and non-objective forms—it is necessary to

10. William Blake, *The Body of Abel found by Adam and Eve, c.* 1826. Tate Gallery, London. (See colour plate 148)

10

dispense entirely with the cause-and-effect theory of history which underlies most art-historical accounts of the development of our culture. A true appreciation of the influence of occultism will be gained only when the role of hermetic schools in the periodic revitalization of culture is clearly grasped. There is as yet little evidence of this becoming a living reality in academic circles.

The essential thing about occult art is precisely that it is *hidden*. The occult artist works with secrets, and carries his secrets, formulae and structures to a deeper level than ordinary artists usually do. He may work in this way for a number of reasons—for example, because he is commissioned to restrict his imagery and meanings for a small coterie of esotericists, as was Botticelli (figure 6), or he might hide his meaning because he worked for individuals who had no real wish to be persecuted or burned as heretics, as did Bles (figure 8), and perhaps Bosch (figure 9), or he might have painted a 'hidden' meaning in a personal attempt to reflect upon the superficiality of the modern culture which has lost contact with the hidden worlds (figure 12)—yet whatever the reasons, his very method of working leads to an important question in the appreciation of this art. One may ask, how is it possible that an occult work of art, a hermetically-sealed cosmic truth, is recognized as such by the art historian? How does one discover the key to the secrets within an image, before one even knows of the existence of such a key? In what way does the art historian pierce the hidden symbolism which has been intentionally designed to fool other men?

The answer to such questions is that very often he does not. In those few cases where an occult work is recognized in its true depth this is often a result of patient research, supported by a not inconsiderable knowledge of occult and heretical lore, yet one may be certain that for every occult work revealed, a thousand must go unrecognized.

My own study of this hidden art has led me to observe a strange phenomenon, which is that the subtle hall-mark of the true occult artist is that he will leave a slight chink in his armour, presumably to encourage an approach to his work by the non-initiated. All occult works of art known to me are designed in such a way as to lead the sensitive observer to suspect the presence of some hidden meaning: the real occult artist gently leads the sensitive spectator towards his secrets with delicate hints and guesses.

In most cases, this is done with a few slight misplacements of symbolism, a tiny hint within the structure of the work, some obvious defect in the pictorial unity, which

11. Wassily Kandinsky, *Battle*, 1910. Tate Gallery, London.

12. Max Ernst, *Of This Man Shall Know Nothing*, 1923. Tate Gallery, London. (See colour plate 192)

11

12

13. Zodiacal Pisces, from the West front of Amiens Cathedral, 13th century.

14. Pisces: detail of marble zodiac in floor of San Miniato al Monte, Florence, dated 1207. (See figure 2)

13

14

leads the alert spectator to ask questions. Usually, the answers to these questions lead to the unravelling of an ancient mystery. For example, the detective work involved in seeking out the dual mystery of the hermetic structure of San Miniato in Florence, which is grounded in the secrets of zodiacal Taurus and Pisces took several years. A simple question led eventually to the secret connection between the worshipper, the orientation of the church, the floor of the nave, the ceiling of the apse, the movement of the sun, and the presence of Christ, the whole bound up in present time, yet with a particular constellation of planets over eight hundred years ago—all this was developed from a single clue within a detail of zodiacal symbolism in the marble zodiac. I had found myself asking why the sign of Pisces was presented in an image of two *parallel* fishes, instead of in the traditional image, important to the nature of Pisces, of two fishes swimming in opposite directions (figures 13 and 14). The unravelling of the mystery took some years and over twenty visits to San Miniato—and perhaps even now the full depth of this mystery centre has not been fully explored or revealed.

In many cases the detective work leads to traditions far removed from conventional understanding, and it has not been possible to explore these to advantage. An example of this may be seen in figure 15, which is linked with the Rosicrucian stream of the esoteric Grail legends, and which may be understood only by those familiar with the ancient Zoroastrian dualism which pervades occultism. The 'hints' are found in the letter M of *Melshisedec*, which is in a rare mediaeval form which is also the ancient astrological glyph for zodiacal Leo.[11] This solar sigil is placed over the Host, the body of the Christ, which is also a solar disk. This requires that the curiously displaced C which terminates the name is also a crescent Moon, itself over the 'Grail' of the Chalice by which the solar Blood will redeem the world. A quite new view of occultism would be required to grasp and explain such profound symbolism.

The occult artist does not speak directly, but issues a nuance of symbolism towards the spectator. Perhaps this in itself reveals the most profound side to occult art—that it is not an art wallowing in obscure hermetic symbolism, fantastic cosmic visions, and fanciful conceits, but an art patiently awaiting the questing eye of any mind which already feels, with that powerful lucidity of the subconscious, a secret and hidden matter, patiently waiting to be revealed.

15. The high-priest *Melchisedec*: capital in the nave of the Cathedral of Saint Pierre, Geneva, 13th century.

THE LIVING BULL

A secret symbolism of the mediaeval zodiac

ACCORDING TO THE occultists, the gothic cathedrals are repositories of an arcane wisdom. The modern esotericist Ouspensky, giving a journalistic sketch of Notre Dame in Paris, reflected upon the contrast he felt between the depth of knowledge expressed within the cathedral's structure, and the somewhat superficial knowledge of modern man. He maintained that the cathedrals expressed in stone an ancient science, in knowledge now hidden to man:

> By the end of the first thousand years of the Christian era the monasteries had gathered all the science, all the knowledge, of that time. But the legalisation of the hunting and prosecution of heretics and the approach of the Inquisition made it impossible for knowledge to reside in monasteries.
>
> There was then found or, to speak more accurately, *created*, for this knowledge a new and convenient refuge. Knowledge left the monasteries and passed into Schools of Builders, Schools of Masons . . . The schools within presented a complex organisation and were divided into different degrees; this means that in every 'school of masons' where all the sciences necessary for architects were taught there were inner schools in which the true meaning of religious allegories and symbols were explained and in which was studied 'esoteric philosophy' or the *science of the relations between God, man and the universe*, that is, the very 'magic' for a mere thought of which people were put on the rack and burnt at the stake.[1]

This idea of a hidden 'esoteric philosophy' is an old one among occultists, who have at all times recognized that numerous hermetic symbols, from elementary magical signs to massive cathedrals, are repositories of an arcane wisdom. The need for such occult devices and structures arose not merely from a wish to preserve secret knowledge from heresy hunters, but also because occultists understand that certain forms of knowledge simply cannot be

16. Portal within the narthex of the basilica of Vezelay, France, 12th century.

17. Detail of Pisces fish from the archivolt of the left door of the West front, Chartres cathedral. (See figure 46)

imparted in the ordinary way, through written books, or even by oral communication. The knowledge of certain secrets can only be earned, sometimes through suffering, sometimes through effort, and at other times through secret meditative practices.

However, the cathedrals were intended to speak many languages, and whilst it is certainly true that many of the cosmic secrets expressed within their forms are still hidden from ordinary eyes, it is also true that certain levels are becoming more accessible to modern man. In particular, the streams of knowledge expressed through astrological imagery are becoming clearer.

Very many of the masonic secrets were expressed in zodiacal imagery, not merely because the ancient astrology was itself a hermetic reservoir of arcana, but also because the zodiac, placed, according to the mediaeval image, beyond the furthest planetary sphere of Saturn, was itself a suitable image of the higher spiritual worlds. This fact alone explains why so many of the Romanesque porches have the zodiacal signs displayed upon the archivolts, for the upper half of the door-curviture symbolized the celestial spheres above man, in both a physical and moral sense, whilst the two doors before man, on a level with his corporeal being, symbolized the duality which colours the familiar material world of experience. Many of the Romanesque portals are designed around a structure which in its simplest form is an encircled *tau*—the 'Egyptian Cross'  which no less a Saint than Paulinus of Nola[2] listed as one of the important images of the cross of Christ (figure 18).

This encircled *tau* may be drawn over the top of the lovely twelfth century portals of the narthex of the basilica at Vezelay (figure 16), the upper segment enfolding the tympanum, and the divided lower segment enclosing the two doors of the portal. The foot of Christ rests at the centre of this 'secret' geometry, touching the top of the *tau* cross, in a symbolism which is linked with the esoteric tradition attached to Pisces. The upper spiritual area of the encircled *tau* contains the judgement of Christ, which is in turn enclosed by the archivolts which depict scenes from the so-called Shepherd's Calendar, and the signs of the zodiac.

Below, the duality of choice in the material world is symbolized in the two doors.[3] On these massive doors are huge metal knobs, wrought into the forms of lions' heads, bearing rings in their mouths. The circle of the archivolts continues its invisible circumference directly through

18. The *tau* structure of the main portal of the West front of Autun Cathedral.

these knobs, linking their forms with the celestial world, and pointing to a hidden symbolism. These lions are visual references to the lion of Judea, King David, by virtue of whose progeny the body of Jesus was prepared to make possible the descent of Christ into the flesh. These lions' heads are silent testimony to the fact that, just as Christ descended into the material world through a 'lion', so must we humans, now on the point of entering the cathedral, do so by means of a lion. The lions' heads unite us on the physical world with the Christ of the spiritual world above.[4]

Such zodiacal symbolism as the roundels in the archivolts, and the position of Christ's foot, and the secret geometry of the encircled *tau* (figure 18), relating to the descent of the Christ, may scarcely be described as commonplace, but in fact such symbolism is extremely common in mediaeval art. Without an awareness of such occult forms, a great deal of the inner significance of the cathedrals—and of the mediaeval world map (figure 20)—will be lost.

In the second century Clement pictured John the Baptist as surrounded by thirty followers or disciples.[5] This number corresponds approximately to the days of the month. Clement was of course aware that all months do not contain exactly thirty days, so in order to indicate a less precise figure than thirty, he included in the group circling St. John a woman, who was (as Clement puts it) 'only half a man'. This play on the weakness of woman, which would raise such an outcry nowadays, was taken very seriously by the church writers, who were later to trace an etymology for the word *foemina* ('woman') from *fe minus*, 'less in the faith', an entirely fanciful etymology raised to encourage witch-finding.[6]

This lunar circuit of twenty nine and a half followers around St. John was then contrasted unfavourably with the twelve disciples who stood around Christ. The number twelve was chosen because this is the number of zodiacal signs, linked in the popular mind with the twelve months, so in this imagery Clement was merely following an established literary and iconographic tradition, itself rooted in occult lore, which links Christ with the Sun.

Christ was more than once described as the solar centre of the solar system, with the zodiac set around him in adoration, and it is probably such imagery which sanctioned for centuries the uses of zodiacal circles in churches and cathedrals—a practice which was in effect a continuation of pre-Christian architectural principles.

19. The encircled *tau*, which combines the unified spiritual world with the duality of the material world.

20. Description of the geography of the world within an encircled *tau*: a 13th century world map from a manuscript in the British Museum.

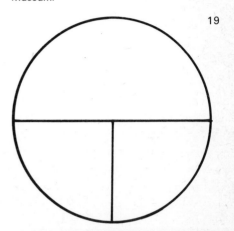

19

20

This important link between Christ and the Sun led inevitably to the use of zodiacal imagery to express His nature. In particular, a link was drawn between Christ and the zodiacal sign *Pisces*, a relationship which will be examined more fully at a later point (page 33), but a no less important connection was made between Christ and the zodiacal *Taurus*.

The associations attached to Taurus are especially rich, but on the whole they are grouped around the idea of *incarnating spirit*, of spirit made manifest through materiality. On the one extreme such associations are seen in the Taurean idea of the *Logos* or Word descending into the physical body; at the other extreme in the popular astrological tradition which gives Taurus rule over the human voice and singing (sound or word made manifest)—a rulership which has encouraged one modern astrologer to trace a fanciful link between the sigil for Taurus ♉ and a schematic picture of the human larynx, with the Eustachian tubes leading to the ears.[7] This concern with incarnation explains why Taurus is so often linked in astrology with the creative act, since from an occult point of view the artist stands as a mediator between spirit and matter: he is the channel through which spirit finds expression on the physical plane. Astrologically, this role of Taurus may be expressed by saying that whilst Aries deals with unmanifest spirit, Taurus acts as a funnel for that spirit, which by means of the alchemical process of creative Taurean incarnation, finds expression or manifestation in the next sign Gemini. In this primal order, Aries is pure spirit, Taurus is the formative force, and Gemini that which is communicated.

It was precisely the connection between the heavenly *Logos* and the material sound which lead Origen to suggest that Mary conceived Jesus through the ear; a suggestion which produced a curious iconography of the Holy Ghost as a small bird whispering into the ear of Mary. An interesting late example of this simple link between Taurus and the Word is found in a carving on the back of a wooden pew from Naestved Church,[8] which in a line of Latin repeats the word *Verbum* with the penultimate letter U in the form of the sigil for Taurus: VERB ♉ M. This important symbolism, which links Christ the *Logos* with zodiacal Taurus, permeates much of the occult and hermetic streams of mediaeval religious art.

The image of Taurus the bull has also a connection with the four Evangelists, each of whom were from the very earliest times symbolized by zoomorphic forms. Whilst

21. Christ crucified, surrounded by the tetramorphs of the four Evangelists. From a 13th century manuscript in the British Museum.

22. The four fixed signs—Taurus, Leo, Scorpio and Aquarius—after a woodcut of the zodiac and planets by Peurbach, *c.* 1515.

Matthew is presented as a human with wings, Mark is a lion, John an eagle, and Luke a bull. These zoomorphic forms are precisely those of the four fixed signs of the zodiac. The human of Matthew is that of *Aquarius*; the lion of Mark is that of *Leo*; the eagle of John is that of *Scorpio* (for which the 'unregenerative' image is also a scorpion);[9] whilst the bull of Luke is that of *Taurus*. Once this symbolism is seen in its full implication one may begin to understand why the mediaeval artists were so fond of placing the four zoomorphic figures around the crucified Christ (figure 21), for in so doing they indicated that the *Logos* contracted into space and time from the outer periphery of the celestial spheres wherein the zodiac lies. In this respect such images resemble the basic horoscope figure, which in its simplest form is that of a cross within a circle: ⊕ The cross itself marks the precise point in space and time at which the incarnating spirit appears in the new-born body, whilst the outer circle symbolizes the zodiacal circle, or pure spirit. As in Aristotelian metaphysics, the circle represents the movement of pure spirit, whilst the cross represents the movement of sublunary materiality.[10]

Thus, even by the fourth century, Jerome was merely gathering together ideas already old when he drew a link between the four Evangelists, the four seasons, the four elements, and the curious tetramorph of Ezekiel's vision, which has remained the conventional explanation for the zoomorphic forms of the Evangelists ever since.[11]

Naturally Jerome was anxious to find the prototypes for this important Christian symbolism within the hallowed confines of the Old Testament, yet in fact the same iconography has an astrological origin, and is found within Babylonian astral teachings which influenced the present notion of the zodiac.

In the same century that Jerome was writing, the less thoroughly Christianized Julian the Apostate was reluctantly revealing that there was an important difference between the astrology of the Mysteries and the astrology of the astronomers, between 'what the Gods or mighty daemons teach the priests' and what the astronomers construct as 'plausible hypotheses from the harmony they observe in the visible spheres'.[12] This contrast between the 'secret doctrine' astrology, as one historian[13] calls it, and the hypotheses of the astronomers has been a common enough theme in the history of occultism, reaching a culmination in the brilliant, if obscure, works of Blavatsky.[14] The contrast is expressed in the conflict between the esoteric and exoteric teachings preserved within the Christian Churches. Thus, whilst the exoteric forms of astrology were generally frowned upon and even rejected by the Church,[15] for reasons which now seem obscure to us, the esoteric forms and traditions were everywhere embraced, and became the very basis of Church symbolism. The survival of the esoteric tradition concerning the four fixed signs of the zodiac, and their relationship to the Cherubim and to the four Evangelists, so puzzled the exoteric historians of Church symbolism, that they were reduced to far-fetched literary analogies to explain the connection between the image of the Bull and the Evangelist St. Luke, failing to see the obvious link between St. Luke and the bull of Taurus.[16]

In discussing ideas ascribed to Orpheus, the Christian Athenagoras described the figure of what he called *Chronos Ageraos* (unaging time), who 'was a snake with the heads of a bull and a lion, between which was the face of a god. On his shoulders he had wings. . .'[17] This hybrid has been linked with the old Persian *Zervan Akarana*, but whatever its ultimate derivation, it is clear that in the four separate images we have a single tetramorph to which the later astrological imagery of the four Evangelists may be traced.

The Evangelists are animal-headed because they are linked with the 'Living Ones', the Cherubim of the zodiac,[18] and specifically with the four fixed signs of the zodiac, so that one modern art historian may claim that

    beneath the bull, lion, human and eagle faces of the cherubs are concealed the zodiacal signs of the solstices and equinoxes and perhaps the four main elements of matter.[19]

The esoteric use of the Evangelist-zodiacal symbolism is found most consistently in baptistries and church pulpits. This is perhaps to be expected: the idea of baptism is connected with spiritual birth and incarnation, and is therefore linked directly with astrological concepts, whilst the pulpit is connected with the idea of the dissemination of the word of God, with the larger question of the *Logos*, and is frequently linked with the image of Taurus, the ruler of the human throat in the image of zodiacal man (figure 24).

One of the most remarkable of esoteric pulpits is in the tenth century *pieva* of San Pietro at Gropina, a hillside village outside Loro Cuiffena in Tuscany.[20] This early pulpit has a lectern composed of a vertical triad of the face of a lion, a human being and an eagle (figure 26).

23. Details of the tetramorphs from the illumination at figure 21 — in descending order, Matthew (Aquarius), Mark (Leo), John (Scorpio) and Luke (Taurus).

24. Zodiacal man, from a 15th century *Shepherd's Calendar*.

24

Separated from this triad by a line of spiral and foliage interweavings, there is a line of triangular motifs, probably intended to symbolize the trinity, and below these twelve *orans* (praying) figures, almost certainly the twelve disciples, ranged around the top of a curious double column.

The interesting thing about the vertical lectern triad is the absence of the symbol for the fourth Evangelist, St. Luke, for whom one might reasonably expect to find a bull's head. In fact, whilst this bull's head is not clearly in evidence, a careful examination of the details of carving reveals that one of the ten triangular forms above the head of the twelve disciples is actually in the form of a bull's head (figure 25). This small head has not been relegated to an obscure position without some conscious intent on the part of the designer, and in fact the larger 'bull's head' is invisibly contained within the lectern trinity. Each time the priest ascends the Gropina pulpit to preach to the congregation his own human face is elevated above the group, and figures as the 'missing' fourth symbol, as he speaks the Word of God. Through this zodiacal symbolism the priest is directly associated with St. Luke, and becomes a personification of Taurus the Bull, as representative of the living *Logos*!

The lovely marble pulpit in the basilican church of San Miniato in Florence has a frontal lectern triad remarkably similar to that in Gropina (figure 29). This pulpit is of twelfth century workmanship, and consequently is less archaic in style, yet it shows the same relationship of Scorpio, Aquarius and Leo, presented in a way which permits the transformation of the priest into the image of a Logos-bearing Taurus.

With the example of Gropina in mind, one might expect to find a trace of bull symbolism in the pulpit itself, yet no such symbol is to be found. The presence of a mithraic image on the tomb of the Cardinal Jacopo of Portugal in the nearby chapel might, because of the connection with the bull, suggest some pervading heretical link, for all the differences in time.[21] However, it is neither to the pulpit itself, nor to the bull image on the mithraic design that one must look for trace of this 'missing' bull, but to the large marble zodiac in the floor of the nave (figure 2).

It is, of course, not the *presence* of the Bull on this zodiac which explains a connection with the pulpit—a zodiac without Taurus would be a very imperfect zodiac indeed. The secret connection between Taurus and the pulpit is to

25. Detail from the pulpit in figure 26 opposite, showing triangular motif of the bull's head, above the figure of an *orans*.

26. The 10th century (?) pulpit in the pieva of San Pietro, Gropina, in the district of Arezzo.

27. Detail from the South transept of Pisa Cathedral: the bull is probably *c.* 1160.

28. General view of the *Piazza dei Miracoli*: the Baptistry is *c.*1153 onwards, but with a Gothic crown; the Cathedral was enlarged *c.*1160 onwards, the Campanile was begun *c.* 1174, but not finished for nearly two centuries.

be found in the precise relationship which this image of a bull holds to the rest of the church. This bull image is so related to the orientation line of the nave that it lends an almost sublime meaning to the image of the missing 'Word' implicit within the pulpit.

In order to grasp the significance of this placing it is necessary to reflect upon the practice adopted by the cathedral designers in orientating their buildings to the East, which has been (with a few notable exceptions) the standard practice from about the sixth century.[22] This Eastern direction represents an orientation 'towards sunrise', a fact which appears to have embarrassed not a few early Churchmen, on the basis that it linked Christ directly with solar imagery and therefore savoured of pagan sun worship. It is for this reason that Christian literature tended to emphasise the idea of an Eastern orientation as being required by ritual because the worshipper was facing Paradise, which was generally believed to be in the East.[23]

In this context, the term 'East' is rather misleading. So far as the orientation of buildings is concerned, this is a fairly imprecise direction, for architects drawing up the line of orientation required to know precisely to which part of the East the building should be directed. William Durandus, writing in the thirteenth century (by which time the practice of Eastern orientation was firmly established) gives several alternatives which satisfy ecclesiastical requirements.[24] He appears to take it for granted that the very act of orientation arises from an urge within man to find his place in the cosmos, and that the church itself was erected as a kind of intermediary between man and the invisible cosmic world, whose laws are known through the movements of the celestial bodies. He expresses this concept in his directive that the 'head of the Church must point to the East, to that point of the Heavens at which the sun rises at the equinoxes'. He rationalises this choice not by development of the obvious (though perhaps heretical) concept of a 'solar' Christ, but by reference to the fact that this precise point symbolizes the *moderation* of the church, since at the equinoxes the days and nights are equal and balanced. It is for this symbolic reason that he insists that orientation should not be directed towards sunrise at the solstices, when the day or night is longest—though significantly he admits that this is indeed sometimes done by church masons. He fails to observe that there is yet another common Eastern orientation, which aligns the axis to the point of sunrise on

29. Detail of the lectern of the 12th century pulpit in the basilica of San Miniato al Monte, Florence.

29

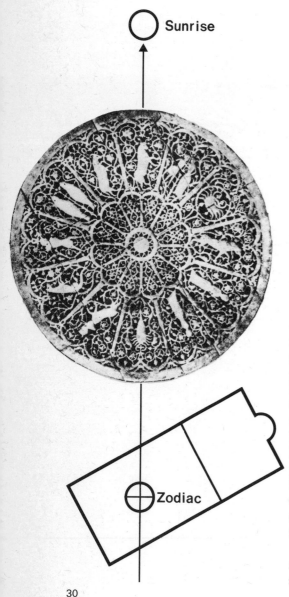

30. The orientation of the floor zodiac in the nave of San Miniato al Monte, which directs the sign Taurus towards the arc of sunrise over Florence.

Sunrise

Zodiac

the Feast day of the patron saint who presides over the edifice.

Now, the whole point about the orientation of the basilica of San Miniato is that it is *not* orientated in any way to the East. The sun does not rise at the east end of the Church, which is properly speaking not the 'east end' at all. San Miniato openly breaches all the fundamental rules set out by the masonic tradition: this naturally suggests that there is some hidden purpose in their defection from the tradition.

The mystery of San Miniato's orientation is linked with an aspect of zodiacal symbolism which will be studied at a later point (page 42), yet at the same time it is linked with the orientation of the floor zodiac in the nave. The remarkable fact is that this zodiac is so related to the body of the church that the sign for Taurus is itself directed towards the East. The missing bull of the pulpit is marked by the daily rising of the sun, which is greeted by the eastward looking Taurus (figure 30).

This zodiacal orientation is directed towards the rising sun as a visual and philosophic completion of the imagery contained within the pulpit, for it points, in its esoteric way, to the solar Christ who incarnated into materiality for the supreme Sacrifice. This blood of the Logos is spilt in much the same way as the bull of the mithraic mysteries, that it might by the sacrifice regenerate the entire earth upon which it runs. Between them, the pulpit and the zodiac proclaim the mystery of the incarnation of the solar *Logos*, and link with traditions older than Christ.

Such considerations as these explain why in so many crucifix images the bull of St. Luke, which is the exoteric form of Taurus, is placed at the bottom of the cross, at the feet of the crucified figure. Not only is this the lowest point of incarnation, but it is also the place at which the blood flows on to the earth. In some figures the feet of the Christ are literally nailed over a chalice, the receptacle for the Holy blood, recalling directly the relationship between the sacrificed Christ and the bull's blood of the Mithraic rites (figure 31). In yet other images the chalice is placed below the feet of Christ, and above the image of the bull: in the example from East Jutland (figure 32), a crescent moon has been incised on to the metal leaf, as part of the decorative motifs next to the chalice: the moon is the receptacle for the sun.

In fact, this precise orientation of Taurus in this marble zodiac is linked not merely with space—albeit cosmic space—but also with time. This beautiful zodiac is actually dated within the intarsia decoration with the year 1207. Since the practice of dating such works was not widely practised in mediaeval art,[25] we may assume that there may have been some purpose in giving a zodiac, which is linked with all time, if not with all space, a particular year.

In view of the relationship which the zodiac holds to Taurus one may not be over-surprised to find that on May 28th, 1207 there was a conjunction of five planets in the constellation of Taurus![26] It would have been a great temptation for the builders of the marble floor to grasp this exciting (and rare) conjunction as an opportunity to extend their Taurean symbolism of orientation which links the solar Christ with the sun, to a perfect link with the whole constellation of Taurus.

The baptistry at Pisa contains a famous pulpit by Nicola Pisano which exhibits similar features to the two from Gropina and San Miniato. Though the 'classical' quality of this work places it in an entirely different class, the astrological associations within its structure are just as evident for the practised eye (figure 33). Pisano, instead of constructing a simple lectern support in the earlier tradition, has grouped the symbols for Leo, Aquarius and Scorpio on different levels around the pulpit. The winged eagle of Scorpio supports the lectern slab; this is in turn supported by a complete winged human figure, which is standing upon a column resting upon the back of a lion. Whilst it is still possible to read into the significance of this grouping the idea of a priest as representative of the living bull, the Taurean *Logos*, the consequences of interpretation are more complex than in the previous two examples.

The bull is not especially well hidden in this pulpit, for Pisano has carved a small figure of a calf in the talons of the eagle (figure 34). This is in itself an interesting device, replete with occult significance, and one is compelled to ask why this Evangelist figure should be portrayed as powerless within the context of baptism. The answer to this question surely lies in the fact that a person brought for baptism is in a Christian sense 'powerless': Christ is not yet a living force within his being. Baptism itself represents a 'second birth' when spirit is allowed to penetrate into the materiality of Taurus. Pisano's pulpit is so placed as to overlook the immersion font, and it would therefore be reasonable to expect that somewhere in the vicinity there should be a symbol of a *living* bull, representative of the *Logos* of the solar Christ.

This living bull is found outside the baptistry, on the

31. Roman Mithraic relief—the slaying of the bull, surrounded by images relating to degrees of initiation.

32. Detail from the base of a 13th century crucifix in the National Museum, Copenhagen.

31

32

33. Detail of lectern from figure 34: the eagle of St. John with a dead calf in its talons.

34. Nicola Pisano. Pulpit in the Baptistry at Pisa, *c.* 1260.

35. Quentin Matsys (or follower of), *St. Luke Painting the Virgin and Child, c.* 1510. National Gallery, London.

33

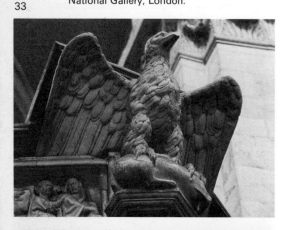

34

walls of the duomo, opposite to the baptistry. On the right-hand side of this immense building is found the only piece of sculpture which juts out from an otherwise unadorned wall—a bull which leaps out feet-first into the skies (figure 27), almost in imitation of the traditional image of Taurus. This bull is leaping upwards and outwards in proclamation that spirit has succeeded in entering into matter, and thereby regenerating the lower forces within the new Christian.

In the baptistry, the bull is dead; in the duomo it is alive and striving upwards. In the third building, the famous leaning tower of Pisa, which is the campanile, this Taurean impulse is transformed into pure sound as the vocal chords of the bell tolls the Word of a spiritually charged message into the surrounding air.

The progression from the dead bull to the living bull, and then to the living sound is upwards, from the earthbound font, mounting half-way up the duomo walls, and then up to the very top of the campanile, to the bells arranged in the twelve arches of the top storey (figure 28). In terms of spiritual progression there is a movement from dead matter, to the union of spirit with matter, and then to the liberated spirit of pure sound: this movement towards spiritualisation is a reversal of the incarnation of the *Logos* who is first pure spirit, then crucified (in the very cruciform image of the duomo), and finally dead. Baptism is within this rich context of the *piazza dei Miracoli* seen as a striving to reach up to the spiritual world by the way of Christ, which explains why the bull emerges, like the blood spilt from the side of Christ, once dead, but now triumphantly alive.

In such Logos-Taurean imagery as one finds in Pisa, San Miniato and Gropina, one begins to sense something of the depths of the connection between the ancient star-wisdom and esoteric Christian symbolism. This depth should not obscure the fact that the link between the incarnation and the Bull has left various exoteric traces in European art, for which no ordinary explanation is available.

Most notable among these survivals is the esoteric connection drawn between St. Luke and the arts. St. Luke is indeed the patron of the arts, a fact which is virtually impossible to explain without recourse to occult symbolism. The traditional explanations for this curious choice of patron are not altogether satisfactory: for example, the popular notion that St. Luke was a painter, and the first artist to make a picture of the Virgin, may be dismissed on the grounds that much evidence has been gathered to show that he was a physician and could not have been an artist.[27] Needless to say, the icon tradition which is said to have been derived from St. Luke's images indicate iconographic and theological concepts which point to an origin several centuries later than the known lifetime of the Evangelist. The legend of St. Luke as portraitist of the Virgin is in fact no older than the sixth century.[28] And yet, in the exoteric and esoteric tradition this Saint Luke is regarded as patron saint of the arts, and is frequently depicted in this role, accompanied by the attendant bull, which underlines his connection with the mysteries of Taurus (figure 35).

This tradition of St. Luke as artist is explicable within the terms of astrological symbolism. This second sign of the zodiac (Taurus) is said to be fructified by the pure spirit of the preceding first sign (Aries)—by this means spirit incarnates into matter. Aries is the 'fire' of spirit, whilst Taurus is the 'earth' of matter. In this symbolism, spirit descends into matter, to find expression on the material plane of ideas (the third sign Gemini). Thus, in terms of astrological doctrine, the invisible world of pure spirit descends into the inertia of Taurus, and manifests as creative activity on the human plane. The creative act is always and everywhere the result of the struggle of pure spirit with the recalcitrant materiality of Taurus, in order to give manifestation to the ideal. It is therefore especially suitable that a bull, which stands four-footed between the spiritual ideal (Aries) and the expression of the idea (Gemini), should be associated with the arts. In a sense, therefore, it may be said that St. Luke is patron of the arts by virtue of the astrological association he holds with the fixed sign of the zodiac.

This idea of the Taurean impulse standing as a point of intersection between spirit and matter is superbly expressed in the details of the pulpit at Gropina, for the twelve figures of the disciples (those humans who followed the *Logos*) are carved in the curious *orans* gesture, with nipples and navels clearly marked. In this form they represent a double image of bull and man, their raised hands in imitation of the bull's horns, and their nipples the bull's eyes (figure 26). This bull symbolism is further enhanced by virtue of the circle of twelve disciples being on level with the human face in the church itself, reminding one that above is the spiritual sphere, from which descends the *Logos* spirit. That *Logos* symbolized by the bull on earth, the Bull in the skies, and the sound of the human voice.

35

36. Meister des Marienaltars, *Two Maries*
(?), The German National Museum,
Nuremberg.   36

DUAL PISCES

The heresy of the two Jesus children in mediaeval art

A STORY TOLD by Julius Africanus recounts how the three Magi, after they had sought out and worshipped the Jesus child, had His portrait painted. They then dedicated this picture in one of their temples, and inscribed it with the title, *Jupiter Mithra*.[1] Jupiter and Mithra are, of course, two quite separate 'personages': Jupiter is a planetary ruler, with dominion over the zodiacal signs Sagittarius and Pisces, whilst Mithra is the ancient Iranian sun god.

The story is interesting because it suggests a dual nature for the Jesus child in a way reminiscent of an old heretical idea which claimed that there were in fact two quite different Jesus children, both born into the physical world by different mothers, and both charged with the preparation of special bodies for the coming incarnation of a single Christ.

The symbolism in the panel at figure 36, and the twelfth century ivory relief at figure 37, is rooted in this ancient tradition. In the ivory at figure 37, the two Jesus children are of different ages: the child being adored by the Magi is much older than the other one, still in swaddling clothes in the crib, looked over by the ox and the ass. This older child is fit to be worshipped by 'Kings' or 'Magi', whilst the younger one, born in a secret place, is visited by shepherds of lowly state. A similar contrast is seen in a more subtle symbolism in figure 36, for the Meister des Marienaltars has pointed to a difference not so much through age, as through dignity shown in the various halos. The halo of the left-hand Mary is richly crowned, that of the child at her feet is more ornate than the child at the feet of the other Mary. The symbolism implies that one child is of Royal, the other of humble, birth. This imagery, and related symbolic forms, intended to express the different origins and purposes of the two children, is a remarkably common theme in Christian art, though its occult and heretical connections have on the whole been missed by art historians.

37. Detail of ivory relief of the Nativity and the Coming of the Magi, 12th century, probably Italian. Victoria and Albert Museum, London.

37

38

This idea that there were two Jesus children is at first hearing quite absurd, for it confronts our most fundamental religious prejudices, yet it is an idea supported by the Gospels themselves. The Gospels of St. Luke and St. Matthew are the only two canonical records of the birth of Jesus, and yet both quite clearly refer to two different children.

In the Luke account[2] the child is born in a humble manger in Bethlehem (the family in fact lived in Nazareth), and is visited by shepherds. His father Joseph was the son of Heli. This Jesus remains in Nazareth, save for an annual visit to Jerusalem. The lineage of the child is traced by Luke back to the priest Nathan, at which point the genealogy merges with that of David.

In the Matthew account[3] the child is born in Bethlehem, where his parents lived, there being no mention of a manger. His father Joseph was the son of Jacob. This Jesus is visited by Magi and afterwards, in order to avoid being murdered, is taken by his family to Egypt: after the death of Herod they return not to Bethlehem, but to Nazareth. The lineage of this child is traced by Matthew back through a quite different scion to Solomon, at which point it too joins the house of David.

The problem of the two different genealogies represents one of the numerous difficulties which theologians term as 'Synoptic Problems'[4]—they in fact represent a duality of births which no honest textual ammendation may reconcile in one personage. It is inevitable, in view of this, that even in exoteric religious literature the idea of two Jesus children has survived. The third century Pope Hippolytus refers to Jesus as 'both king and priest in one person'[5] with reference to the tribes of Judah and Levi, a theme which has been given to no less an authority than Thomas Aquinas.[6]

In some of the so-called apocryphal literature the idea of a double Jesus is also explicit. For example, in the third century Gnostic *Pistis Sophia*, which the historian James quite rightly describes as 'just readable',[7] are passages which are in fact perfectly readable and crystal clear if the idea of two Jesus children is accepted, in place of our more familiar notion. For example, in one beautiful passage there is a moving account, given by one of the Maries, of how she confused her own son's double:

When thou was little, before the Spirit came upon thee, the Spirit came from the height whilst thou wast in a vineyard with Joseph, and came unto me in mine house in thy likeness, and I knew it not, and I thought that it was thou. And the Spirit said unto me: where is Jesus my brother, that I may meet with him? and when it spake thus unto me, I was in perplexity, and thought that it was a phantom *come* to tempt me. I took it therefore and bound it to the foot of the bed that was in mine house, until I should go forth unto thee and Joseph in the field and find you in the vineyard, where Joseph was staking the vineyard. It came to pass then, that when thou heardest me tell the matter unto Joseph, thou undestoodest the matter and didst rejoice, and say: Where is he, that I may behold him? Otherwise I will tarry for him in this place. And it came to pass, when Joseph heard thee speak these words, he was troubled; and we went together and entered into the house and found that thou wert like unto him: and he that was bound to the bed was loosened, and embraced thee and kissed thee, and thou also kissedst him, and ye became one.[8]

Various Zoroastrian texts make direct reference to the dual Messiah idea,[9] but especially interesting are the numerous references in the Dead Sea Scrolls.[10] Modern scholarship wanders around this 'double Jesus' material in faint bewilderment, reducing the idea to the fusion of political and sacerdotal roles in one Messiah.[11] Similarly art historians have tended to miss the Gnostic strains of the heresy, because of their willingness to treat the double appearance of the Luke and Matthew Jesus as examples of 'continuous representation'. Once the nature of the heresy is clearly grasped, this modern interpretation must in many cases be dropped. Naturally the double-Jesus image was merely an 'iconographic tradition' by the early mediaeval period, and in most instances there may be little doubt that the esoteric truth was not recognized, any more than those who used the familiar *Christmon* ☧ realised that they were using a sigil which linked both with the Egyptian *tau*, a symbol of life ♀ and the Greek abbreviation for *Chronos*,[12] manifest Time: ☧

The double-Jesus iconography insists on an age difference between the two young children, especially in regard to the so-called nativity scenes. In fact, there are two quite different traditions, which have been fused together by a failure to understand the implicit dualism— the nativity scene is concerned with the Luke child, whilst the adoration of the Magi is concerned with the Matthew child. In almost every case, the two children are presented at different ages: the occult tradition insists that the two children were not born at even approximately the same

38. Ivory relief, with the Adoration of the Magi and a manger scene based upon the apocryphal account of the *Protevangelium*. 6th century, Gnostic. The British Museum, London. (See colour plate 54)

39. Detail of panel from the 12th century *Golden Altar* in the National Museum, Copenhagen. The adjacent panel shows the coming of the Magi.

40. Detail of panel from the 12th century *Golden Altar* in the National Museum, Copenhagen: the Luke Jesus in the manger.

39

36

41. Details of relief from the 8th century Pemmo Altar, in the Cathedral Museum, Cividale.

time. The Gospels also make this clear.

The Luke Jesus was born when Joseph and Mary went to Bethlehem to be taxed—'And this taxing was first made when Cyrenius was governor of Syria'.[13] The Matthew Jesus, on the other hand, was born 'in the days of Herod the King'.[14] Herod, who received the Magi of the Matthew Gospel, and who tried to murder the infant, was himself dead by the time Cyrenius was made governor of Syria. Therefore, as Heidenreich points out, even in terms of straightforward history, the Herod story comes *before* that of the shepherds.[15]

Ormond Edwards, who has investigated the chronology of the Gospels with considerable insight, comes to the conclusion that 'a clear impression is created that each nativity is a distinct and historical fact'.[16] On literary and astronomical grounds, he places the Matthew Jesus about a year before the Luke Jesus, the former birthday being 4 January 1 BC, the latter being 25 December of the same year. Curiously enough, from the beginning of the fourth century the Church celebrated the feast of Christ's nativity on the 6 January, and only later changed to the present date.

This important difference in the ages between the children is generally indicated in those paintings and sculptures which depict the two Jesus children. For example, in a sixth century ivory, probably Coptic in origin (figure 38), the upper register has a child in the arms of Mary which is clothed, and bearing a scroll. He is obviously much older than the Jesus child in the bottom register, who is still wrapped in swaddling clothes.

Very many examples which demonstrate the age differences could be given,[17] though one or two images present the two children at later stages in their ages, at which point the differences in stature and clothing is not apparent. For example, the marble relief from the right-hand side of the Pemmo altar at Cividale (figure 41) shows the Jesus children of approximately the same stature, as does the famous painting by Borgognone in S. Abrogio, Milan. In this latter case the Luke Jesus is twelve years old, the Matthew Jesus thirteen, even though they are painted almost like identical twins.

The esoteric tradition concerning the two children was not reserved for obscure ivory reliefs of a Gnostic character, and curiously enough does not appear to have died away as the Church Triumphant built a formidable machine against dissent and heresy. On the contrary, the imagery of the double Jesus appears in several landmarks

41

42

42. Detail from the tympanum of the left door of the North portal at Chartres, 12th century.

43. Tympanum of the left door of the North portal at Chartres Cathedral, with the adoration of the Magi in the top register, the story from the St. Luke Gospel in the lintel register.

43

38

44. Detail from the archivolt on the right door of the West front at Chartres Cathedral—the zodiacal signs Cancer and Aries. (See figure 45 below)

45. The right door of the West front at Chartres Cathedral, which has only ten signs of the zodiac within the archivolt.

46. Detail from the archivolt of the left door of the West front at Chartres—the zodiacal Gemini and (almost hidden by the pediment) the fish of Pisces. For a detail of this Pisces symbolism, see figure 17, page 17.

44

45

of Church art and architecture, not least of which is Chartres cathedral. A beautiful double grouping is found on the tympanum above the North porch (figures 42 and 43), with the Jesus of the Magi much older than the Jesus of the Shepherds. An extensive visual commentary on this 'double Jesus' theme runs through the entire cathedral.

The huge thirteenth century windows of the north apse, which are of course above the outer fabric of the porch (figure 43), expresses the genealogical record of the two Jesuses, and in so doing presents the imagery of the two Virgins for which Chartres is famous in occult circles, and which is seen as a recapitulation of the ancient Egyptian teachings concerning Isis and her dark sister Nepthys.[18] In the enormous rosette of the window is the Virgin with the child on her lap. Around this centre are outer roundels depicting the twelve kings of Judah, a somewhat obvious theme of the 'royal' line of descent.[19] Under this rosette are five lancet windows, the central one of which shows the 'black Madonna', named Saint Anne,[20] with the Infant on her arm. The four adjacent lancets show Melchisedek, David, Solomon and Aaron. This arrangement is a peculiar one, and it is designed to reflect the dual line of *priest* and *king*, which meet in the single incarnation of Christ. This group depicts two pairs of king and priest, side by side.

To the right of the black Virgin are the two lancets with Melchisedek and David. The writer of the Epistle to the Hebrews links the priestly Jesus with Melchisedek, who combines kingship with the high priesthood. In greeting Abraham returning from the slaughter, he became a type of priesthood, linked with the house of Levi: 'Thou *art* a priest for ever after the order of Melchisedek'.[21] The kingship of David, in the side lancet, is emphasised by placing his figure over the dying Saul, from whom he took royal command of Israel.

To the left of the black Virgin are the two lancets with Solomon and Aaron. Once more there is the kingly line— Solomon being son of David and Bathsheba, the 'wife of Urias' in the genealogy of Matthew.[22] Aaron represents the priestly line, for he was chosen to become high priest through the miracle of the flowering rod in the tabernacle—'the rod of Aaron for the house of *Levi* was budded. . .'[23]

This mystery of the two Jesus children on the outer fabric of the building, supported by the references to the two genealogies on the inner stained glass, comes to an almost incredible summation in the stonework on the

Royal portal, the main entrance to the cathedral. In the archivolt above the right door, images of the so-called 'labours of the months' alternate with the signs of the zodiac. The order of this zodiac is not correct, nor is it complete. There are only ten signs represented: the two missing ones are Gemini and Pisces (figures 44 and 45).

The significance of the displacement of these two zodiacal signs is of paramount importance to the theme of the two Jesus children, and links with the most profound of all esoteric doctrines concerning the duality. For these two symbols are to be found, isolated from the rest of the zodiac, on the left-hand door of the Royal portal, alongside a recapitulation of the 'two Jesus' imagery. In this large tympanum the highest register shows the child in the lap of Mary, who wears a crown, evocative of the 'Royal' line of the Matthew Gospel. In the lower register we have the 'priestly' Jesus, not only visited by the Shepherds, but also on a cradle which is standing on an altar.

The archivolts around this tympanum are taken up largely with the traditional symbolism in which the seven liberal arts are allegorized and their famous exponents portrayed. Entirely out of context with this symbolism, at the left-hand foot of the archivolt, are the two displaced signs for Gemini and Pisces (figure 46). The two children are standing behind a single shield, the pointed tip of which is directed to the fish below. This peculiar, and indeed unique, presentation of Zodiacal imagery[24] may be explained, and related to the two Jesus children imagery, only by reference to the esoteric tradition concerning the origin of the names and symbolism for the signs Pisces and Gemini.

It has been claimed that the names and associations for Virgo, Gemini and Pisces were determined by Mystery Schools long before the birth of Christ, in anticipation of His coming.[25] The Virgin birth is expressed in the image of Virgo, the young woman who holds the ear of corn, the binary star *Spica*: some mediaeval astrological images show the Virgin holding the ear of corn in one hand, the Child in another; others show her dress decorated with corn-heads (figure 50).[26] It is no accident that our Virgo was the ancient *Ceres*, that the magician Albertus Magnus gave the ascendant of Christ's horoscope to the sign Virgo, and that the sigil for Virgo (♍) has been traced by some scholars to the letters MV, *Maria Virgo*.[27]

The two children were figured in the sign *Gemini*, destined to be born of Virgins. This explains why the

46

47

48

earliest images of the Gemini show two young boys embracing (or even conjoined in one physical body): only in the late mediaeval tradition do they sometimes become male and female.[28]

Pisces, the dual fishes, is the sign of the solar Being who will incarnate in the specially prepared body. The profound mystery which links Christ with the fish image has not yet been adequately studied or treated, and the somewhat dry academic suggestion that the fish symbol is merely a result of an interpretation of a Greek acrostic[29] is superficial in the face of the true profundity of the esoteric truth.[30] The historian of esotericism de Mely came to the conclusion that the fish carried a talismanic reputation long before the Christian era, so that it is apparent that the fish imagery must have been adapted for specifically Christian purposes.

The Piscean imagery of Christ runs throughout mediaeval art, and it is often noted with satisfaction that the Virgin faces the Christ (*Pisces*) across the zodiacal skies, in pre-Christian times an image of the Virgin derived from Isis mythology, in post-Christian times an image of the Virgin birth, with the double Gemini standing in quadrature to both Virgo and Pisces.[31] The link between the image of two children and two fishes is nowhere more forcefully expressed in art than in the two details of the magnificent doors of San Zeno at Verona (figures 47 and 48), the first of which shows a woman suckling two fishes from each of her breasts, the second of which, in much the same gesture and position, suckles two children.[32]

Of course, the question which arises from a study of the two genealogies and the related works of art is, *why* should two Jesus children be required to prepare a single body for the coming Christ?

An answer to this question is very complicated, and an approach to a solution would require some familiarity with the esoteric view of the nature and destiny of man. However, it is possible to give some general indication along the lines of Rosicrucian occultism set out by Steiner,[33] as well as by reference to cabbalistic teachings, which postulate a dual Adam.

According to this tradition the two Jesus children represent the two different aspects of the original dual Adam which had to be united in one body, if the incarnating spirit of Christ was to redeem the world. There was on the one hand the Adam who descended deeply into matter, the 'terrestrial' Adam, called *Protoplastes* in cabbalistic literature, whilst there was on the other hand the 'Aziluthic' Adam, *Adam Kadmon*, the 'celestial', Adam *Illah-ah*, as he was variously called.[34]

The Luke Jesus, the one from the line of the priest Nathan, was the bearer of the pure unadulterated soul of the *Adam Kadmon*. The Matthew Jesus, the one from the line of Solomon, was the bearer of the soul of the terrestial *Protoplastes*. This Adam had the name which meant 'earth'. Interestingly enough, this idea of the Solomon line being connected with 'earthly' incarnation is contained in the Jesus genealogy set out by Matthew, for it lists four women, three of whom, as Jerome himself admits, were immoral.[35]

It is surely this union of purity and sin, of the Celestial and the Terrestrial, in the union of the two Jesus children, to which Paul refers in his *Epistle to the Ephesians*, when he reminds his correspondents that man is brought to God through Jesus Christ, who united the lusts of our flesh with grace: 'to make in himself of twain one new man, *so* making peace; And that he might reconcile both unto God in one body by the cross. . .'[36]

In a sense, the descent of the *Logos* united in one form the two spiritual elements represented by the Jesus children. This idea is graphically expressed in the astrological sigil for *Pisces*, which may be exoterically explained as consisting of two curves representing spirit and soul united by the 'silver cord', and esoterically by the single *Logos* uniting the two qualities of *Adam Kadmon* and *Protoplastes* (♓).

The association between Christ and the Age of Pisces has been widely recognized by occultists and historians, even if there is no agreement as to when this Age ends, and the new one begins. The imagery of the fish as symbol of Christ (figure 52) was widespread, and as we have seen from the example at Chartres, was used even in esoteric contexts. The sigil for Pisces was sometimes used to symbolize Christ, as may be seen from a striking survival in the south ambulatory floor at Christchurch, Hampshire. Here, in one of the epitaphs dedicated to a former rector of the church, the name *Christchurch* is spelled in abbreviated form with the sigil for Pisces representing *Christ* (figure 49). In fact, the precise form of this sigil is relatively modern, for it first appears in manuscript form in the early 14th century.[37] It is quite possible, therefore, that the very same mystery schools which were carving images of the two Jesus children, and linking these with the age-old Piscean tradition, also put into the world an image for Pisces which links the two curves (two fishes,

47. Eleventh century bronze panel from the main door of the church of San Zeno, Verona.

48. Detail of woman suckling two fishes from the bronze panel in figure 47.

49. Detail of 17th century grave slab, from Christchurch, Hampshire, with glyph for Pisces symbolizing the name *Christ*.

50. 15th century wood print of Madonna, with ears of corn upon her dress. National Museum, Copenhagen.

49

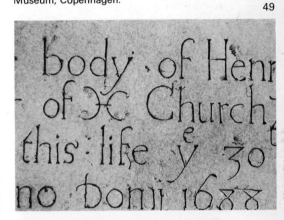

50

42

two Jesus children?) into one single form, thus with one stroke transforming the Greco–Byzantine sigil for Pisces, which had a related form)(.

The most complex use of Piscean association with Christ is to be seen in the mystery centre of San Miniato, which has aready received some attention in regard to the *Logos* and Taurean imagery. This basilica is of ancient design, with the choir raised over the crypt, which contains the body of San Miniato, believed to have been beheaded in Florence in the third century. Within this building are several levels of occult symbols and devices, including one of the largest marble zodiacs in Italy, as well as a zodiacal pulpit (figure 29).

The presence of a floor zodiac in a Christian building may puzzle those unfamiliar with the nature of mediaeval symbolism. The fact is that Christian art never entirely rejected pagan symbolism, and rarely managed to give astrological teachings more than a surface coating in adapting it for specifically Christian needs. The reason for this may be observed in the writings of Aquinas himself, for he does not dispute the power of the stars, but merely says that they exert influence on the lower man.[38] In addition to this, there were distinct heretical and occult streams running through the masonic tradition, not to mention a powerful pagan/alchemical symbolism which ran as an undercurrent beneath the mainstream of standard religious symbols.[39]

In relation to the zodiac, which was at one time a common item of mediaeval church decoration and symbolism, the rationale behind its presence was the fact that the basic zodiacal structure, which united in one form the circle with the cross, symbolized one solution to the basic mediaeval problem which was expressed in exoteric form as 'the squaring of the circle' ($\oplus$). The encircled cross was the conventional symbol of the basic Christian architectural form which, as Burckhardt puts it, 'perpetuates the fundamental diagram of the cross inscribed in the circle' and which is 'at the same time the symbol of the Christ and the synthesis of the cosmos'.[40] The circle expresses the totality of space, the spiritual world, whilst the cross inscribed within it represents the divisions of time and space, mediating as it does between the circles of the sky, and the square of the earth. The horoscope is a figure intended to symbolize the descent of spirit to earth (literally, out of the space and time—the zodiac), and its re-assent at death: it is a graphic expression of the inbreathing and outbreathing of life. The zodiac is

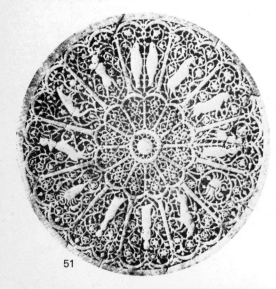

51. Marble floor zodiac, dated 1207, from San Miniato al Monte, Florence.

52. Gnostic relief of the 4th century—the fish as symbol of Christ. British Museum, London.

51

52

53. Apse mosaic of Christ enthroned, in San Miniato al Monte, Florence, *c.* 1297.

54

therefore a symbol in miniature of that alchemical process by which spirit enters matter—the esoteric aspect of the 'squaring of the circle'. In its cosmic aspect, rather than in relation to the microcosmic, it is therefore a most convenient symbol for the Christ.

It was a fair commonplace for mediaeval writers to compare the cruciform plan of the church to the prone body of the crucified Christ. His head was the apse, the transepts His arms, the nave His torso and legs.[41] The floor zodiac, therefore, may be seen as a symbol of the solar Christ descended into the earth for the salvation of man, a symbol at once of sacrifice and redemption, the two key themes of the sign Pisces.

The Piscean imagery of the 'dual fishes' runs throughout the length of the basilica of San Miniato, starting, conveniently enough, at the zodiac floor. In this zodiac the remaining eleven signs are symbolically presented in a manner which does not significantly deviate from basic astrological symbolism: the symbol for Pisces is not presented in its traditional form. Instead of the two fishes being presented as swimming in opposite directions, connected with the line which is usually called 'the silver cord', these two fishes are unconnected, and face the same direction (figure 56). This variation from the norm must have been intentional on the part of the masons, particularly as the floor zodiac of approximately the same date in the Baptistry in Florence shows the two fishes in a glyph of traditional united form. It would appear that these two San Miniato fishes were orientated in this direction, and unconnected by any line or cord, in order to draw a visual connection between the zodiac and the two similar fishes which are to be found as marble inlay on the wall which separates the choir from the nave, up the steps over the crypt.

On this wall the two fishes are quite separate (figures 57 and 58), the space between them designed for human access to the choir: they are also on level with the human face, which in looking towards them will see between their forms the altar. This position reminds one of an early Christian mosaic, which shows two fishes alongside the bread of life (figure 55). The symbolic intent at San Miniato is to indicate a connection between the Pisces imagery in the nave zodiac, which is on level with the feet of the worshipper, and these separated fishes which are on level with his head. The lower part of man—what mediaevalists would have called the demonic—is raised to the rational man.

54. Gnostic ivory relief, *c.* 6th century, with the Adoration of the Magi, and in the lower register, a scene from an apocryphal account of the birth of Jesus. British Museum, London.

55. Early Christian mosaic, with two fishes and bread on the altar. In such contexts, the fishes are linked with Pisces, the bread with the opposite sign Virgo.

56. Detail from the floor zodiac in San Miniato al Monte, Florence. See figure 51.

55

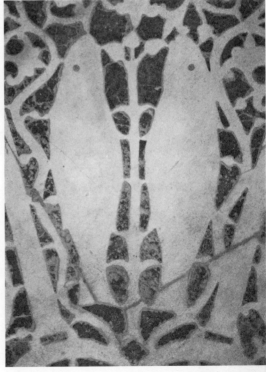

56

57

57–58. Details of the two walls separating the raised altar from the nave, in San Miniato al Monte. 13th century.

58

This progression, upwards in a physical sense, and outwards in a spiritual sense, is continued in the apse of the basilica, and takes one up over the head of the worshippers. This time one is no longer confronted with the form of a dual fish, but with a symbol which is just as ancient as the fish in its association with Pisces. In the cupola of the apse is a lovely thirteenth century mosaic which depicts Christ in Majesty, surrounded by the four fixed signs of the zodiac, usually called the 'four Evangelists'. To the right of Christ is Mary, and to His left, the martyr San Miniato (figure 53).

The magic of this third range of Piscean associations is worked by light itself. At certain times of the year, towards the end of the day, a stream of sunlight falls from an upper clerestory window, and moves slowly across the bottom of the apse mosaic, in an arc towards the Christ, until it lights up exactly the shape of His foot. The curious pattern of the foot is *exactly* covered by the patch of light: then, after a few moments of ecstatic golden vibration, the light spreads out over the lower part of the mosaic and dissipates itself.[42]

A fantastic precision of design was required to engineer this miracle. The fact is that the position of Christ's foot within the curved arch of the mosaic, the angle of the clerestory window—even the angles of the tesserae which compose the foot—are so related to the orientation of the Church, and the movement of the sun, that the solar disc at infinity touches the lowest point of the solar Christ portrayed in space and time. This curious phenomena must have been engineered with more mathematical precision, and with infinitely greater sense of aesthetic, than that used by Cassini half a millenium later to use the sunlight in the Basilica of S. Petronio in Bologna.[43] It is significant of the change in human consciousness which took place in those centuries that the architects of the esoteric school at Florence should present solar orientation to express a profound mystery regarding the *Logos*, whilst a later mathematician should use church orientation to record the transits of the sun, without reference to its spiritual significance.

That the mediaeval masons should go to such lengths in order to light up the foot of Christ is itself of great significance, for the foot of the human form is itself ruled by Pisces. It is for this reason that the majority of images of the so-called zodiacal man (figure 61) show two fishes either over or alongside the feet. When in San Miniato basilica the sunlight turns the tesserae of the feet into an

59. Detail of Christ in Glory, from the apse mosaic of San Miniato al Monte. (See colour plate 53)

59

area of shimmering light, the intention is to express the most highly spiritualised concepts of Piscean symbolism, for it is at once uniting the sunlight with the Sun *Logos*, the lowest part of this *Logos* with the highest part of man, the splendid vibrant colour of the apse with the quiet darkness of the nave zodiac.

The progression of the Piscean imagery through the basilica is inwards and upwards, both in a physical and in a spiritual sense. In the physical sense, the worshipper is required first of all to look down, in order to examine the glyph for Pisces at his feet. Later, when he has climbed the steps towards the choir, he is invited to enter through the doorway, and thus pass through the body of Christ, level with his own face. Finally, when he has entered the choir, he looks upwards, and far above his own head he sees the foot of Christ, transformed by the very same movement of the Sun which defined the outer perimeter of the floor zodiac, in its yearly course against the fixed stars.

In the spiritual progression, the symbolism is concerned with light. The marble floor of the nave is lighted by the diffused sunlight which finds its way with difficulty into the basilica. In this sense, the Piscean image is at man's feet, near to him, yet a symbol of the sun and the zodiac which are as distant as the fixed stars. The marble fishes on the choir wall receive more daylight from above, and since these are level with man's face, and quite visible, they may be regarded as being 'humanised', and certainly are less remote than their prototypes on the floor: Christ is no longer on the distant earth, but is now intrinsically bound up with man's own perceptual being. At this level man has chosen to ascend the steps towards the altar, and finds himself participating in the body of Christ, standing between the two separated fishes. The third Piscean image depends for its force entirely upon the influx of sunlight from the heavens, which with miraculous aim moves over the foot of Christ (figure 60). This is the transmuting, healing force of the spiritual world, which may be seen only if one looks upwards, into those planes higher than the ordinary level of existence. In this third level of Piscean imagery, the remote sun of the zodiacal ecliptic has come to earth, and through its link with the foot of Christ, becomes the lightened version of the Pisces at the foot of man in the dark nave. It is an image of almost unfathomable depth, for it unites within its cycle the macrocosm and the microcosm, the everlasting zodiac and the transient human experience.

60. The three Piscean elements within the internal design of San Miniato: the fish of the zodiac (bottom left); the fish of the altar wall (bottom right), and the two feet of Christ.

61. Zodiacal Man, from a 16th century manuscript, *The Guildbook of the Barber Surgeons of York*. British Museum, London.

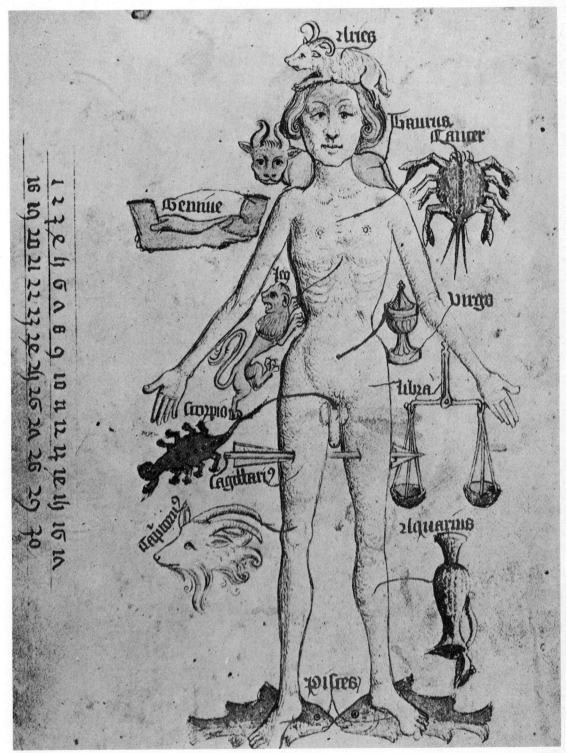

62. Francesco del Cossa and Cosmè Tura,
the so-called 'Month' fresco, relating to
Taurus, in the Schifanoia Palace, Ferrara,
c. 1470.

MERCURY OF ANGELS

Hermetic symbols in Renaissance art

RENAISSANCE ARTISTS AND thinkers resurrected a past which their scholars believed to be rooted in the ancient knowledge of Egyptian magic, but which in reality was a less ancient continuation of Greek speculative thought.[1] The first important text which the humanist Ficino translated from Greek for his patron Lorenzo was not from the Platonic canon, but from the hermetic school of Alexandria: significantly, both Ficino and Lorenzo believed it to be more ancient than Plato, and even related to the wisdom of Moses.

Whatever the antiquity of their sources, a powerful new hermetic wisdom was distilled from such documents, and a fascinating occultism was brought to life in humanist Florentine circles. Yet the fact remains that the major Renaissance themes, for all their conscious return to past mythology, was deeply rooted in astrological and hermetic teachings which were so popular in their day as to be scarcely noticeable as 'ideas'. These occult ideas were presuppositions—one might even call them 'prejudices'— which inform Renaissance art so thoroughly that unless we seek to understand them, the true meaning of many of its greatest works will remain hidden from us.

The occult and astrological tradition was strong in art and literature: the famous book on magic compiled by the youthful Agrippa at the end of the century, *De Occulta Philosophia*, was little more than a compilation of sources already old, and familiar material to most of his scholarly contemporaries.[2] The once-legendary astrological fresco by Giotto in the Palazzo della Ragione in Padua was an enormous compendium of astrology—and this in a university town in which no less a person than Pietro d' Abano lectured in astrology: this stood firmly at the head of the Renaissance. Shortly afterwards Tura and Cossa painted the half-lost decanates in the Palazzo Schifanoia in Ferrara (figure 62), drawing in Arabian and mediaeval symbolism images the meanings for which are now

63. The twelve exoteric images of the zodiacal signs, from a 15th century German ephemeris.

63

obscure but which are far from 'traditional', and probably are derived ultimately from ancient Egyptian astrological ideas transformed by Arabic concepts.[3]

The image of the *sign* Taurus (top right, figure 63) is instantly recognizable in the star-studded *constellation* Taurus in figure 62, yet they are from different traditions, the latter from the Egyptian decanates, perhaps in this fresco given a conceptual basis by Pellegrino Prisciani, who taught astrology in Ferrara contemporaneously with the artists Tura and Cossa.

Such hermetic astrological images remind us that the occult traditions were complex and wide-spread both before and during the Renaissance. In the following century, Peruzzi conceived a vast astromythic fresco for Agostino Chigi in Rome, surely the largest personal horoscope in the world, yet modern scholars argue even about the fundamental nature of the figure upon which it is based.[4] Such masterpieces as these are the iceberg tip of a tradition which floundered to an end in the obvious dilletantism of the occult and astrological symbolism of Vasari, perpetrated on the walls and ceilings of the Palazzo Vecchio in Florence. In between Giotto and Vasari virtually every occult idea found a secret niche in Renaissance art.

The great Renaissance artists transmuted the occulta of the past, and from it distilled new iconographic qualities in an art form which is almost incomprehensible without a full knowledge of the astrological, magical and hermetic beliefs in which the period was submerged. Our very familiarity with certain works is almost a result of prejudice, for we are constantly seeking to recreate Renaissance art in our own image. In doing this we may at times achieve a pleasing aesthetic titillation, but we certainly miss many of the real profundities which Renaissance art has to teach.

A striking example of this 'prejudicial blindness' may be seen in the contemporary attitude to one of the most famous chalk drawings of that period, the so-called *Virgin and Child with St. Anne and St. John the Baptist*, recently abbreviated to 'The Burlington Leonardo' (figure 64), both titles of which impede our understanding of the drawing, and indeed limit our comprehension of its real meaning. Little is in fact known about the drawing, though an informed guess places it around the year 1505.

The official title appears to be definitive, and indeed it satisfies all but the most penetrating examination, since it is well known to art historians that the subject of the St.

64. Leonardo da Vinci, *The Virgin and Child with St. Anne and St. John the Baptist*, c. 1505. National Gallery, London.

65. A page from a 17th century manuscript on astrology, in the Public Library, Lucca. The manuscript lists the towns and countries and their zodiacal rulerships. Florence (*Fiorenza*) is ruled by the sign Aries.

66. Early 16th century wood-carving, probably St. Anne with the Virgin Mary and the Jesus Child. National Museum, Copenhagen.

Giovannini, 'little St. John' was established in the previous century as a subject for painting. Such a theme also had much relevance for a Florentine artist, since St. John is the patron saint of that city, the ecclesiastical usurper of the pagan Mars, who lorded it over Aries, the zodiacal sign which to this day presides over Florence (figure 65). And yet, this is not a title which Leonardo himself gave to the drawing, and the subject matter indicates that it belongs not to the St. Giovannini tradition, but to that concerned with the two Jesus children imagery.

An examination of the drawing within the context of this esoteric tradition resolves one or two problems within the imagery. For example, the curious merging of the two female bodies, a theme which is introduced more than once by Leonardo, and one which has been given a rather superficial explanation by Freud,[5] may be seen as a prefigurement of the merging of the two separate Jesus lines: the two mothers become one mother by virtue of the mystery of the Incarnation. There is in fact a mediaeval tradition in which sculptors merge the bodies of the two women—usually within the Saint Anne/Virgin Mary imagery—though this may not have been familiar to Leonardo (figure 66). The unfinished hand of the Mary to the right of the picture is perhaps hard to explain within the 'Giovannini' tradition, but takes on a poignant significance within the framework of the two Jesus imagery: not only does it link the two children compositionally, but it unites them with the spiritual spheres, an indicator between their bodies (joined in Geminian fashion, one notes) of the spiritual spheres from which the single incarnating Christ will descend. It is probably no accident that this upraised hand should have the index finger raised in such a marked fashion, for this finger is ruled in occult lore by the planetary Jupiter (figure 67), which in turn rules Pisces.

In the Leonardo drawing it is significant of the underlying theme of the two Jesus imagery that one child is in the laps of the two women, removed from the earth, whilst the other is kneeling on a grassy bank with one foot on the earth. This is no doubt symbolic reference to the 'Celestial' and 'Terrestrial' Jesuses, a direct image of the Kingly Jesus who is worshipped precisely as a King, and the priestly Jesus, who is of humble birth, and who is often laid directly on the earth, or on rush matting, in mediaeval images.

One may only speculate where Leonardo obtained his knowledge of this heretical tradition, which we nowadays relate to 'esoteric Christianity', but which even in the sixteenth century would have been quite heretical. Perhaps he had the secret from Ambrogio Borgognone who lived in Milan whilst Leonardo was there: this painter was certainly aware of the tradition in its most subtle form, for he had painted a most moving fresco which showed the two children in the Temple.[6] However, a tradition which was heretical, even before the reaction set in from the Council of Trent, is unlikely to have been reported openly in preserved documents, and the source of the tradition in Renaissance thought is so far unknown. Perhaps Leonardo da Vinci was himself an initiate, a secret adept, and had the knowledge from his own personal insights into the spiritual world.

Whatever the source, the drawing remains a mystery and mysterious. To explain away its immense popularity in terms of its aesthetic qualities, as Lord Clark[7] does, is not only to underestimate the power of the drawing, but also to fail in understanding the deep attraction it exercises on the subconscious mind of the most casual visitor to the National Gallery, London. No great sensitivity is required to realise that in the presence of this drawing one is faced with a profound mystery: yet it is imperative that one sees that the mystery resides not so much in the quality of the draughtsmanship as in the occult truth enshrined within its subject matter.

A further indication of the extent to which occult and hermetic ideas were almost second nature to the Renaissance artists may be seen from an examination of two very different pictures. One is a result of the combination of impeccable painterly skill and much cerebration, and a painting which few art historians would deny an important place in hermetic history—the so-called *Primavera* of Botticelli, which encapsulated the humanist ideas of his mentors. The other is *Tobias and the Angel*, said to be from the school of Verrocchio, a picture which contrasts strongly with the *Primavera*, for at first glance it appears to be a straightforward picture illustrative of a simple biblical story. Both pictures express secret ideas.

Naturally, the new humanism of neoplatonic thought and the 'old' occultism were not the only fields which had well preserved secrets. The mediaeval guild system was founded on highly specialised 'secret' methods and materials, taught to apprentices only after a strict vow of secrecy. In the painting guilds of St. Luke, there were no methods more secret than those relating to the *composition* of paintings: these were involved with complex and

67. The planetary rulerships over parts of the hand—from Agrippa von Nettesheim, *De Occulta Philosophia*, 1531.

68. Andrea del Verrocchio, *Tobias and the Angel, c.* 1480. National Gallery, London. (See colour plate 77)

67

68

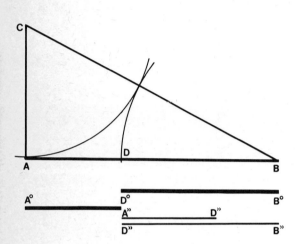

69. The construction of the Golden Proportion.

The Golden Proportion is the ratio obtained when a line is divided in such a way that the smaller part is in the same proportion to the greater part as the greater is to the whole. In the relationship above, D marks the Golden point of the line AB.

The Golden Proportion is constructed on a given line (AB above, for example) by drawing a perpendicular (AC) and marking off on this ½ AB, at C. C and B are then joined, and with the compass point at B an arc is taken from this intersection of CB to cut AB at D.

highly refined geometries in which great emphasis was placed upon the magic significance of the circle, the square, the triangle, and that most mysterious of all ratios, the golden number, called 'the divine proportion'. This proportion is a ratio derived from the unequal division of a line in such a way that the smaller part is related to the larger in the same ratio as the larger to the whole (figure 69).

The reasons why this proportion—of all other proportions—was believed to be 'divine' was set out by the mathematician-monk Luca Pacioli, who wrote a treatise on the proportion illustrated by no less an artist than Leonardo.[8] Pacioli insisted that the ratio was divine because, like God himself, it is unique: additionally, it savours directly of the Holy Trinity in that it is a 'three in one'—three points united in one continuous harmony. He defies even the 'irrationality' of the proportion, on the grounds that just as God is beyond description in words, so is this ratio beyond description in number.

In some respects, Pacioli's book ruptured the tradition of secrecy attached to the use of the divine proportion in studios. This was only possible, however, because the proportion itself was almost out of date—an open secret in the workshops. However, more important to our present theme, there was also the fact that at this time another series of geometric proportions was gaining popularity in artistic circles at that time, and these were still rooted in 'secret lore'.[9]

There is a much disputed passage in one of Durer's letters to his friend Pirkheimer,[10] in which the German artist says that he is leaving Venice for Bologna, where there is someone willing to teach him 'secret perspective'. This secret perspective could hardly be anything to do with ordinary perspective, for by 1506, when this letter was written, there were few things which artists did not know about this geometric art. Piero della Francesca's manuscript on perspective was circulating widely at the time, and the theories of the new art were too well understood in Venice to warrant a special trip to Bologna. Again, this 'secret perspective' could hardly be anything to do with the divine proportion itself, which formed the very basis of mediaeval compositional practice with which Durer was familiar.

It has been suggested that this 'secret perspective' to which Durer alludes was the new *secret geometry* based on the ratios relating to the musical proportions which had been introduced to artists at that time by the great

Renaissance genius Alberti.[11] Sebastiano Serlio, a painter and architect disciple of Alberti, was living in his native Bologna at that time, and would probably have been prepared to teach Durer this art. Certainly this journey which Durer made appears to have had a great impact on his feeling for pictorial space, for on his return to Germany he began to paint and engrave pictures containing the secret musical proportions expounded by Alberti, which had hitherto been used only in Italy. Thus, Alberti's treatment of the Pythagorean harmonics could well have been the 'secret perspective' which he had learned.

There are few Renaissance paintings which illustrate more beautifully the influence of Alberti's principles than Botticelli's *Primavera*, which may indeed be regarded as a kind of visual sermon on the artistic theory of the time (figure 70). Only comparatively recently have scholars succeeded in showing the underlying hermetic symbolism of this painting,[12] so that some idea has been formed of the inner meaning which Botticelli had in mind when he painted it for his youthful patron Lorenzo di Pierfrancesco in 1477.

As with the Leonardo drawing, we are once more presented with a title which misleads. The official title *Primavera* was half-suggested by Vasari, who saw certain figures as symbolizing spring.[13] There is no evidence that Vasari had any idea at all as to what Botticelli intended, yet his suggestion has stuck, and the title itself has led more than one art historian astray.

The real subject of this painting is love, and the creativity which is rooted in love—an important enough theme during the Renaissance. That such is the subject might well be gleaned from the placing of the goddess Venus, the pagan and planetary deity of love, who stands in the very centre of the group, with the blindfolded Cupid above her.

It is significant that this figure should stand a little 'backstage' to the two groups on either side of her, since these two groups represent the dual aspects of love as it was understood by Botticelli, his patron, and that esoteric coterie which shared his ideas. The group to her right represent both ordinary love and contemplative love (in the philosophic sense), whilst that to her left represents creative love, in the artistic sense. The true meaning of these groups is hidden behind pagan imagery and symbolism in a manner doubtless intended to delight the neoplatonic humanists around Botticelli.

Before this symbolic quality in the two groupings may

70. Sandro Botticelli, *Primavera, c.* 1478. Uffizi, Florence (with detail of Venus and Cupid).

70

be fully grasped, it is necessary that we note a particularly exciting and quite original secret structure which underlies the composition of this painting. There are *four* figures to the right of Venus, three to her left, whilst the compositional area which she herself occupies contains two figures (that is, if we include Cupid above her). This number of figures indicates a ratio of 4:2:3, which is precisely the underlying geometrical division of the compositional area.

Figure 71 shows the two major division lines which are calculated across the length of the picture on the basis of 4:2:3. The line to the left of Venus runs precisely down the figure of Flora, so that her foot stands exactly on the important division of the canvas.[14] The line to the right of Venus runs through her own right hand, and separates her and Cupid from the back of the innermost figures of the three Graces. Additionally, the diagonals within this figure partly account for the curious 'backstaging' of the figure, for she fits exactly into the six-sided irregular polygon created by this hidden structure (figure 76).

However, the extent to which this hidden geometry influences the composition itself is not our concern. What is important is that the ratio 4:2:3 is the same musical ratio which in Renaissance times was called the *double diapente*. This proportion, expressing a doubling of 2/3 time, arose from the explorations of Alberti, who influenced enormously the musical theories of Gafurius, as well as Botticelli and several of his contemporary artists.

It should not surprise us that the structure of the *Primavera* is based on a musical proportion, since the goddess Venus was patron of both dance and music, whilst the three Graces move in a solemn yet delicate counterpoint of rhythms to her right, reminding us that they were frequently associated with the music of the spheres, as for example in the woodcut illustrating these themes in Gafurius' *Practica Musicae* (figure 73).[15] This design shows the naked Graces standing to the right of Apollo, who sits at the top of the ascending spheres, each of which emits its own tone of music in accordance with its planetary nature.

The hidden structure of the *Primavera* therefore sets the tone for the entire subject matter of the painting, which proves to be a sermon on the nature of the arts.

The group to the right of Venus expresses the idea of spiritual love. The three Graces have many names, and there are many explanations of their functions, but in Renaissance imagery they have been described as Castitas, Voluptas and Pulchritudo:[16] in this solemn dance of

71. Analysis of the musical ratio of 4:2:3 time upon which the composition of the *Primavera* is constructed. (After C. Bouleau, *The Painter's Secret Geometry*, 1963.)

72. Detail of the *Primavera*, showing the Three Graces.

73. Woodcut from Gafurius, *Practica Musicae*, 1493—the planetary spheres, with the Three Graces to the right of Apollo, a vase of flowers (see detail 78) to his left.

71

Botticelli's conducting they are presented in the traditional manner, with Castitas (who has her back to us) looking towards Voluptas, caught between desire and beauty (Pulchritudo). The theme in this and related groups is that the innocent Castitas is being introduced to love by desire and beauty. Botticelli allows the upper part of her dress to fall down, revealing her delicate left breast on the side of Desire, yet leaves her clothed on the side of Beauty. By this symbolism, he suggests that she belongs partly to both, yet remains still true to herself. The lyrical postures and even the facial expression suggest a constant and eternal exchange between the three elements which underlie the human experience of love: innocence, voluptuousness and beauty.

Mercury is the fourth figure in this group, and his posture and maleness conflict with the sinuous feminine grace of the others: it is this Mercury who offers an escape from the dreamlike dance of earthly love.

In Renaissance iconography Mercury personifies many human and celestial traits, but among the most important of these are those linked with the idea of 'communication with the gods', for which the symbolic aspect are the wings on his feet, which associate him both with the aetherial realms, and with the earth itself. In the astronomical models of the day (figure 75) Mercury was placed between the Moon sphere and that of Venus: thus his sphere was the first one beyond the sublunar, the first entrance into the spiritual worlds.

It is in this role as 'communicator with the gods' that Mercury is presented in the *Primavera*. With his wand he brushes away the cloud in a manner suggestive of the words of the humanist Ficino, who advised Botticelli in these matters, for Mercury is the one who 'calls the mind back to heavenly things through the power of reason'.[17] Through being rooted in the earth, yet free to fly, Mercury has the power to escape from the lure of the three Graces. His role within this four-fold compositional area is an important one, for it proclaims the theme of the picture— that love should have a celestial rather than a worldly aim. Love should attempt to pierce through the clouds which shroud the splendours of the spiritual world from earthly sight. It is this theme which explains why Mercury is reaching upwards and away from the three maidens who represent earthbound love, and also why he is so disinterested in them. It explains also why Castitas should be looking not at her companions, but at Mercury, for it is by finding a balance between love of the

72

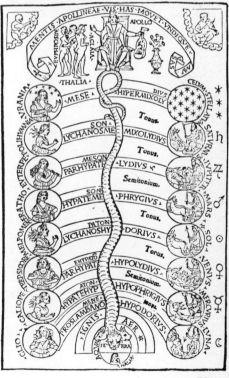

73

74. Detail from *Primavera*—Mercury brushing away the clouds with his wand.

75. The Pythagorean musical ratios, related to the planetary intervals—from Stanley's *The History of Philosophy*, 1660, Vol. III.

76. Double analysis of *Primavera*. The blue analysis shows the arcs which unite the forms with the image of the Pythagorean harmonics. The magenta shows the compositional extension of the rectilinear harmonics of the 4:2:3 time (figure 71).

74

voluptuous and love of beauty that she will reach into that true love which lies in the spiritual spheres, to which Mercury has access.

The central group of Venus and Cupid represents the two polarities of love. Venus is the personification of a love which is restrained and modest (which explains her bearing within the picture): here she is the ruler of all that is gentle, the traditional patron of music and art. Blind Cupid offers a contrast to this gentleness, for he may be taken on one level as representing blind passions.

For all his blindness, however, the aim of this Cupid is precise, and he is releasing his shaft at Castitas, who is thereby required to make a choice: it is the eternal human situation. From the duality which finds a place in every human breast—the gentle urging of Venus and the irresponsibility of Cupid— there arises the dance of human love. This love consists of an exchange between three impulses—that which seeks beauty, that which seeks voluptuousness, and that which attempts to reconcile the two. A successful reconciliation on the earth plane may lead to higher levels, to the so-called Platonic love, through the mediation of Mercury.

The group to the left of Venus exhibits none of this sense of dignified and spiritual calm. The wind-god Zephyrus reaches out for the nymph Chloris, as though making sexual advances. The third figure, dressed in floral robe, is the harbinger of Spring, Flora. The group is an exoteric symbolism: the warm winds breathe upon the earth, and the early flowers of springtime are called into being. The wind blows through the mouth of Zephyrus: the flowers issue from the mouth of Chloris—the unattractively dressed nymph is turned into the beautifully robed Flora. The fact that Chloris and Flora are one and the same person in different bodies partly explains the curious relationship of their forms.

It is the breath of Zephyrus which works the magic— the same breath which would move the clouds above the head of Mercury. The latin *spiritus* means both 'breath' and 'spirit', and within this dual meaning lies a key to the picture. The fact is that Mercury rules human communication and speech, which is maintained at the mouth and lungs. Thus, the imagery of the wind-filled mouth of Zephyrus connects with the staff of Mercury, which is held up in the air. According to the neoplatonic doctrine, the aim of human love was not merely to transcend the earthly, and to reach into the spiritual spheres: it was to return from these spheres, charged with spiritual forces,

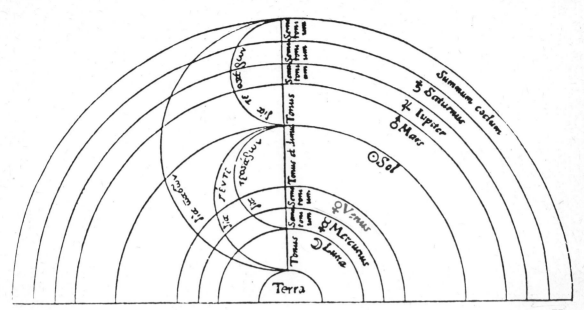

Summum coelum

♄ Saturnus
♃ Iupiter
♂ Mars
☉ Sol
♀ Venus
☿ Mercurius
☽ Luna

Terra

75

76

that they might work through human agency in the world. In terms of this philosophy, Zephyrus represents the human spirit of love which has refreshed itself in the spiritual world, and has now descended back into matter: by working on materiality (Chloris), it is able to transform it into beauty(Flora).

There are two movements within this painting, one of which is visible, one of which is not visible. There is a constant movement across the surface of the picture, from right to left, as the story of the spiritualising influence of Venus is unfolded, and earthly love is transmuted into spiritual love, which in turn descends into matter. There is also an invisible movement from the upwards gesture of Mercury into the spiritual realm (into the space above the picture) which descends in a complete motion into the downward-striving gesture of Zephyrus (figure 76). The apparent structure of the painting is based on the half-circle, which links the upper motion of Mercury with the downward 'incarnating' motion of Zephyrus, through the lip-gesture of Chloris: the upper circle is completed above the picture, in a symbolic form which reminds one that the spiritual world might be said to lie above the physical earth. This 'invisible' symbolism reminds one of those diagrams in the Renaissance texts on music theory, in which such proportions as the *double diapente* are symbolized (figure 75), for the beginning and ending of the various proportions are frequently linked by precisely such a curve which plays no tonal part in the proportion itself.

The *Primavera* is enacted under the sway of this spiritual sphere, for its imagery describes the fructifying quality of the spiritual as it works upon material nature, through the power of love. It is a repeated 2/3 time, in which Botticelli has succeeded in transforming the Chloris of pigment, and binding this material into a Flora of which Venus, as patron of the arts, may well be proud.

Even without an awareness of the occult significance of the Pythagorean harmonics underlying the composition of this painting, and without a knowledge of the astrological link between Mercury and speech, which explains the appearance of the flowers in the mouth of Chloris, a sensitive observer will be aware that it is a mysterious painting. It is what might be termed an 'open secret' that the figures portray some kind of hidden meaning, and it is no doubt this which explains the popularity of the painting in that gallery which is so filled with remarkable works. This sense of imminent secrecy

77. Andrea del Verrocchio, *Tobias and the Angel, c.* 1480. National Gallery, London.

78. Detail of *Primavera*—the descending arc of figure 76—Zephyrus breathes on to Chloris, and flowers sprout from her mouth.

78

naturally prevents the sensitive onlooker from drawing the conclusion that he understands the painting, or has reached into the soul of Botticelli.

This sense of the miraculous is not always evoked by occult pictures, many of which are more elusive with their secrets. An example of this may be seen in *Tobias and the Angel*, said to be by a follower of Verrochio (figure 77).[18] In spite of what a superficial acquaintance with this picture might suggest, it contains a layer of symbolism rooted in occulta, and was indeed in its pictorial intention designed for semi-magical purposes.

The true nature of this hidden symbolism begins to emerge when the painting is set within the framework of the original story of Tobias and the Angel, as abstracted from the *Book of Tobit*,[19] for this reveals that the painting is by no means an accurate illustration to this story.

Tobit, who lived in Ninevah about seven hundred years before Christ, lost his eyesight as a result of a singular accident. It seems that he fell asleep against a wall in the open air, and some hot swallow droppings fell into his eyes, making him blind. Some time afterwards, feeling that his end was near, he called his son Tobias, and instructed him to go to distant Media in order to collect a sum of money which had been left in trust with a friend. He advised Tobias to seek out a travelling companion to accompany him on the long journey, and eventually they both approved of a man calling himself Azarias, who agreed to go with the boy. This Azarias was, however, the archangel Raphael in disguise.

The two companions set out, and eventually they reached the banks of the river Tigris. Tobias waded into the water to bathe his feet, but a monstrous fish[20] leaped out of the water and attempted to devour him. Instructed by Raphael, Tobias managed to catch the fish, gut it, and set aside the heart, liver and gall. Raphael told him that the smoke from the burning of the heart and liver would drive away evil demons, whilst the gall could be made into a salve to heal his father's eyes.

Arriving in Media, Tobias collected the money due to his father, and was introduced to Sarah, with whom he fell in love. A marriage was proposed, though not without certain misgivings, since each of Sarah's previous seven suitors had died on the night of their wedding as a result of demonic activity. It seemed that an evil spirit called *Asmodeus*[21] wished to keep Sarah for himself. In spite of this, Tobias married Sarah, and on the wedding night successfully exorcised the demon with the burning of the

79. George Pencz, engraving of *c.* 1540 from *Tobias* series (with detail of monstrous fish).

heart and liver of the fish (figure 80). The group then returned to Ninevah, and there healed the eyes of Tobit with the fish-gall salve.

By the time that this tempera panel was painted, certain elements within the original story had been changed to satisfy Christian requirements. For example, in the story Raphael was travelling incognito, and under a false name: he was to all intents and purposes an ordinary human being. In the picture, however, he is clearly an archangel, for the wings and halo—even the delicate tread of his feet—leave one in no doubt that the boy is in the company of a celestial being.

This change in imagery lends emphasis to the important theme of protection and healing which runs through the painting. In the *Zohar*, Raphael[22] is said to be the angel charged with the task of healing the whole earth: through his link in the European occult tradition with Mercury, the god of the healing caduceus, the archangel has become a suitable representative of the redemptive *Logos* on earth. Raphael is the mediator who teaches Tobias how to use the fish both to hold back demonic activity and to heal the sick.

A far more significant change within the original story may be seen in the fish which dangles from a string on Tobias' left hand. This is certainly no monstrous fish, but a rather harmless variety of trout. There could be no danger of this little creature swallowing Tobias. To judge from the ancient Assyrian and Persian myths upon which the *Book of Tobit* appears to have been based, the 'monstrous fish' (figure 79) was originally a kind of crocodile, whose heart and liver were indeed standard elements in magical conjurations against demons. By the fifteenth century, however, the iconographic tradition insisted that it was a small fish, and it was commonly depicted as being carried on the end of a string by Tobias. It has survived in this form simply because it is intended as a symbol of Christ (see page 45 and figure 52).[23]

In view of this symbolism, it is probably no accident that directly opposite the eye of the fish held in the hand of Tobias, a fish sigil is painted on the loose belt (figure 81). This sigil is like the common sigil for Christ which has been used from early Christian times.[24] The fish is also linked through occult symbolism with the familiar Pisces, since the string from which it hangs is hooked on the index finger of Tobias, the finger which in the chirognomical tradition is called the finger of Jupiter (figure 67). In the fifteenth century, and indeed until shortly after the

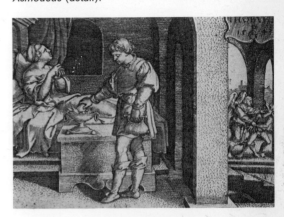

80. George Pencz, engraving of *c.* 1540 from *Tobias* series, in which Tobias burns the heart and liver of the fish, and thus enables the Archangel to overcome the demon *Asmodeus* (detail).

discovery of the planet Neptune in 1846, Jupiter was regarded as the ruling planet of Pisces.[25]

Within this astrological imagery, and its related Christian sigil, the fish is a visual play on the healing power of Christ: the fish is therefore related to the healing power of Raphael, who is the intermediary between Tobias and the *Logos*. This association merely states the opening theme of the picture, however, for a movement may be traced across the entire painting, linking together the human and celestial being in a special way. This rhythmic counterpoint starts out at the left leg of Tobias, takes in the important fish, then up through the *recordo*, the bill held in the left hand, up the arm, through the top swirl of the cloak, down the right arm and into the double twist, where Tobias' hand links with that of the angel. This movement continues in the dart-fold of the angel's cloak, and appears to terminate in the right hand of the angel, which is holding the golden box containing the eye-salve of fish gall. Actually, the movement does not end there, but follows up the cloak-edge of the angel (along the edge which springs from the golden box), along the wing, and up to the head of Tobias, where one finds the rays of an incipient halo, a somewhat curious symbol to find on the head of an ordinary human being.

This counterpoint rhythm began in the Piscean feet imagery, which is rooted firmly in the earth, and terminates at the head, which is linked with the spiritual worlds. Tobias stands between heaven and earth, and is a member of the hierarchy which leads up to the Godhead. This idea of 'hierarchy' is further expressed within the painting by the distinct references to the 'beings' of the mediaeval cosmology. The lowest visible form of life in the physical world, itself rooted in demonic activity,[26] is the mineral world (in figure 82, *lapides*), symbolized in the painting by the scattering of rocks. Higher than the mineral is the plant kingdom (usually *vegetabilis*, but in figure 82, *planta*) shown in the painting in the sprouts of grass and plants. This in turn is lorded over by the animal kingdom (usually the *sensibilis*, but in figure 82 *brutus*), here represented by Tobias' dog, walking alongside the foot of the archangel, and looking upwards towards the fish. Above the animal kingdom comes the human (usually the *rationalita* but in figure 82, *homo*, man), which is of course Tobias himself. Above the human we enter once more into the invisible realm (the invisible realm at the other extreme being the demonic) which is the world of angels, made visible for us here in the figure of Raphael.

81. Detail of fish, from figure 77—the Pisces sigil is about two centimetres from the mouth of the fish.

82. Celestial ladder, from woodcut illustration in R. Lull, *De Nova Logica,* 1512.

82

In the painting the symbols for the lower kingdoms of nature are set in the lower part of the panel: the symbols for the spiritual are contained in the higher. Tobias is supported by the mineral, plant and animal kingdom, and partakes naturally in their being—yet the relationship with the higher spiritual world is a result of his own choice, as the delicate grasp of the angel's arm indicates.

The hierarchical structure implicit within the painting finds several visual counterparts in the symbolic details. For example, the salve box is made of gold and is circular—it is held by the archangel over his heart. For centuries gold, the circle and the heart have been linked with the sun, and it was, as we have seen, a common thing for church writers to compare the sun with Christ. Thus the fish in the left hand of Tobias is transformed (through the connecting counterpoint rhythms) into a golden solar Christ.

Such symbolism reminds one that this panel is a private prophylactic, itself involved with magical praxes, and was intended for a particular journey in space and time, as well as with a visual prayer for 'healing and protection' for an adolescent. During the Renaissance such pictures of Tobias and the angel were fairly common, since well-to-do families would commission such compositions when a son was about to make a long or dangerous journey, or when he came of age. Such a practice was of course involved with an expensive sympathetic magic which called protective forces from both the sacrificed fish (Christ) and the pagan Jupiter, for a young man who was painted in the role of Tobias himself. Such a picture was really a beautiful talisman, designed to ward off evil during a particular journey, or during the special 'journey through life' which he faced. Even in this century there was still a wide-spread feeling for the magical power of 'icons'—not only were astrology and amuletic praxes in full vogue (figure 83), but also pictures of a religious kind were sometimes used for magical purposes. Even as late as 1576 no less a painting than Leonardo's *Virgin of the Rocks* (figure 84) was invoked against the plague, when it was said to have performed the miracle of abating it.[27]

The Leonardo was used as a prophylactic for a whole community: the Verrocchio for an individual, whose identity is now unknown. Both are occult pictures not merely by virtue of the hidden symbolism they contain, but also by virtue of the relationship portrayed within them of the link which man holds with the spiritual world, and with Christ.

83. Magic sigils associated with zodiacal *Virgo*, from the pseudo-Paracelsian *Archidoxis Magica*, 1584 edition.

VIRGINIS.

83

84. Leonardo da Vinci, *The Virgin of the Rocks, c.* 1490. National Gallery, London.

84

85. Berthold Furtmeyer, illumination from the
Archbishop of Saltzburg's Missal, 1481. The
Bayerische Staatsbibliotek, Munich.

SEX SACRED & PROFANE

Heretical and occult symbols connected with the Fall of man and gods

What man is found such an idiot as to suppose that God planted trees in Paradise, in Eden, like a husbandman, and planted therein the tree of Life, perceptible to the eyes and sense, which gave life to the eater thereof; and another tree which gave to the eater thereof a knowledge of good and evil? I believe that every man must hold these things for images, under which the hidden sense lies concealed.[1]

So wrote Origen, one of the first important Christian writers to argue that the Bible was not to be taken literally,[2] and thus opening the way for disciplined theological speculation on the one hand, and for unbridled fantasy on the other. His attitude was rooted in a platonism which was so deeply entrenched in early Christian thought that it has remained a part and parcel of even modern theology: this platonism takes for granted that symbolism, especially that linked with the use of sigils, numbers and secret imagery, is a means by which the material world may be linked with the spiritual. Origen's words, whilst directed at biblical exegesis, could stand for virtually all Christian art up to the end of the mediaeval period, for it assumes that a work of art is an image 'under which a hidden sense lies concealed'.

The most common method of concealment in art was by means of esoteric symbolism. This technique, which ranges from the use of amulets and sigils to direct iconographic analogy, has been closely studied by modern historians. However, there was an equally important and no less common form of occult concealment in art which has tended to attract less attention from conventional historians:[3] this is the use of a complex secret geometry as a symbolic substructure, a 'hidden commentary' on the theme of the work of art itself (figure 86). Such secret geometry was a kind of occult spinal column around which the body of mediaeval art was disposed.

Many of the secret compositional structures of the

86. *Tau* analysis of the 12th century West portal at Autun Cathedral.

87

illuminators, as well as the secret structures of the architects, were intended to present hidden truths in a manner which the symbolizing tendency of the mediaeval mind would grasp on a deeper level than the ordinary level which esoteric symbolism permitted. Three examples of this use of occult geometry may be studied, ranging from a relatively simple construction of the fifteenth century, to highly sophisticated forms in the following century, when artistic practise had to some extent been enlivened by the ideals of the new humanism. Each of the three works we shall examine are thematically linked by solar and lunar imagery, those great universals of hermetic symbolism.

An illumination by Furtmeyer (figure 85) may be taken as an example of esoteric Christian symbolism; a roundel by Henri met de Bles, as an example of a late survival of an heretical secret geometry and symbolism, whilst the large canvas by Tintoretto, *The Origin of the Milky Way*, may be seen as an example of a late use of a sophisticated secret geometry at a time when a non-occult constructional method was already beginning to dominate, if not actually destroy, pictorial composition.

The illumination by Berthold Furtmeyer at figure 85 was painted for a missal given to the Archbishop of Salzburg round about 1481. In the foliage of the tree is the crucified Christ (figure 87), and to the left is a skull (figure 88). From the right-hand side of the tree the queen of Heaven is plucking a 'fruit', the *host*, which normally marks the climax of the religious ritual by which bread is transformed into the body of Christ. To the left a nude Venus plucks the fruit from the mouth of the serpent, which is curled around the trunk of the tree.

In effect, this picture traces one of the consequences of the exegetic treatment of *Genesis*. The tree of the Knowledge of Good and Evil bore a fruit—the *fructus* of the Vulgate.[4] The latin for evil, as used in reference to the tree of Good and Evil, was *malum*, and since this same word meant also 'apple', a tradition developed which held that the fruit of the tree had been an apple. The question of course remained, if the malum fruit was an apple, what was the *bonus* fruit? Furtmeyer solves the graphic problem to which this exegesis gives rise by having the tree produce two fruits.

The evil fruit is linked with the skull lodged in the foliage. A skull is an interesting occult symbol because it is associated both with the idea of death, and with the moon, but it is especially useful in this context because in the

88

biblical account God warns man that if he eats of the tree, then he will surely die.[5] The group of people to whom the *malum* fruit is being given are already under the dominion of Death himself. In general, this imagery links with early Christian texts which claim a connection between the fruit of the womb of Eve (that is, the *malum* apple) and the fruit of the womb of Mary (that is, the Christ). This tree of Eden has been transformed into a tree which symbolizes the conflict between Life and Death—between the lunar forces of evil, and the solar forces of Christ.

This theme of the dual fruits, linked with lunar and solar elements, is developed in this picture by the use of a secret geometry which relates together ideas otherwise unconnected within the illumination. If one places a compass point on the foot of the tree, on a line which runs through the centre of the tree (figures 89 and 90), it is possible to trace an arc which joins the open mouth of the recipient of the Host, with the open mouth of the recipient of the *malum*. The relationship between the placing of the compass point at the foot of the tree, and the termination of the resultant arc in the two hands (figure 90), is probably intended to refer to the tree in its redemptive aspect as the cross upon which Christ died: the two giving hands are nailed to the arms of the tree, the Piscean foot of Christ to the base of the tree. What is significant, however, is the fact that this arc runs directly through the eye of the serpent. This eye is placed exactly half way between the top of the roundel (enclosed within the branches of the tree) and the sexual parts of Adam. This placing of the eye is in itself interesting, for it indicates that the point of temptation (eye of serpent) stands exactly between the highest point of the heavens (the blue sky) and the lowest point of man (the sexual parts from which the snake emerges).

If we place a compass point on the vertical line which runs through the centre of the tree, exactly half-way between the top of the roundel and the bottom of the tree, it is possible to draw a complete circle which runs through the left eye of Venus, through the right eye of the Queen, through the eyes of the skull, and through the wound in the left hand of Christ. At the base it joins together the left arm of Adam to the tree trunk, and to the body of the snake, the tree trunk and the left arm of Adam.[6]

Whilst it is clear that the serpent twisted around the tree is evocative of many alchemical and Rosicrucian images which show serpent power on the tau cross, the real significance of this image is that the tree, the snake and the

87. Christ on the cross—detail from figure 85.

88. The lunar death's head—detail from figure 85.

89. The compositional structure of figure 85.

90. The compositional structure links the 'bread of life' and the 'fruit of death', by way of the mediation of the tree.

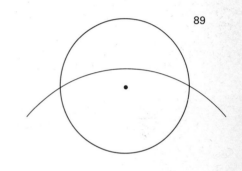

89

90

man all meet at the male sexual parts. This is perhaps to be expected, since the power of the snake is linked with the male sexual powers. Only a most curious dislodgement of perspective permits the left arm of the man to be wrapped around the tree, though this is obviously intended by Furtmeyer to confirm that it is the left-hand side (that is, the *sinister*, lunar side) of man which is at present indissolubly linked with the lower serpentine forces.

The geometry used by Furtmeyer is not intended merely to introduce harmonics into the design, but also to incorporate a series of secret commentaries on the nature of the spiritual world, The eye, which is the theme of this secret geometrizing is both a symbol of the Sun, and of God. It is no accident that if the two systems outlined above are superimposed, then one finds in the very centre of this picture a *tau* cross within a circle, with the upper space occupied largely by the foliage of the tree, and the symbols of good and evil—the horizontal line dividing at once the bodies of the two women, along with the mountain ranges, from the heads, sky and foliage above. This semi-circle is then divided by the vertical line of the *tau* along the two interlinked forms of snake and trunk. The division permits the 'evil' to be on the left side of the design, the 'good' on the right. This distribution is echoed even in the imagery, for the rocks of the mountains behind Venus conflict with the verdant pastures of the right, and the hair of Venus contrasts with the protective cloak of the Queen of Heaven, and so forth. Within this framework, it is significant that the head of sleeping Adam is to the right, for this is a sign of the ultimate regeneration of the Adamic force through the intercession of the solar Christ.

The geometry of Furtmeyer's illumination reminds one of the *tau* magic of the portal (figure 86, page 71): the two occult characteristics of which are the left-hand-lunar, right-hand-solar imagery, presenting the duality of the material world under the eternal unity of the celestial world. This 'duality' of the earth condition—expressed so frequently in the struggle between the angelic and demonic forces of sun and moon—is one of the most constant themes of Christian art. It is found in the earliest of crucifixion images,[7] part of a wide-spread tradition which places Christ between the Sun and the Moon, as an image of Eternal Man on the earth plane (figure 91).

Furtmeyer's hidden symbolism rests heavily on the duality between the good and evil fruits, between the lunar death's head and the solar Christ, both of which are united in the secret geometry by graphic sexual con-

91. Raphael, *Crucifixion, c.* 1503. National Gallery, London (with details of sun and moon 'wrongly' orientated).

91

notations. The hidden theme is that it is in man's sexual urges that the struggle between the lunar demons and the solar angels reaches its greatest pitch. The image is a graphic expression of the conflict between the 'natural' and the 'spiritual' man, which lay at the roots of all the major Christian revivals—orthodox and heretical—in the middle ages.

In the thirteenth century, the Beguine Mechthild of Magdeburg set down a lyrical view of the spiritual love in the Garden of Eden, before the Fall of Man. God had given Adam the chaste and gentle virgin Eve:

> Their bodies were to be pure, for God did not make for them a dwelling of shame, and they were clad in the garments of Angels. Their children were to be engendered in a spiritual manner, as the sun plays upon the water and gives it sparkle, yet without troubling its surface.[8]

But this ideal of virginal conception was not to be realised in Eden, for the pair ate of that terrible fruit:

> When they ate of the forbidden food, then shape descended into their bodies, and made them unclean, as it is for us now. Had the Holy Trinity formed us like angels, so would we by virtue of this angelic nature have no need to be ashamed.[9]

This uncompromising view of the human body as an unangelic thing was, for all Mechthild's connection with the Beguines, orthodox throughout the Church, and supported the idea that sex itself was something 'unclean'. The need for sex was recognised as the stirring of the 'natural man', who had to be supressed by those who sought for spiritual development: beliefs based on opposite points of view came rapidly into confrontation with the Church itself, and were inevitably stigmatised as heretical. One of the propositions condemned as heretical in a bull issued by Clement V in 1311 was that 'Sexual intercourse is not a sin when desired'.[10]

In view of such an entrenched position it is not surprising that a Carmelite friar on trial for heresy in Cambrai in 1411 should have made a statement which led directly to the flames:

> That the natural sexual act could take place in such a manner that it was equal in value to a prayer in the sight of God.[11]

This friar was one of the leaders of the heretical sect known as the Adamites, linked with the heresy of the Free Spirits, who according to their detractors worshipped in naked-ness in imitation of Adam. The knowledge we have of the

92. Albrecht Durer, woodcut from the *Apocalypse* series, *c.* 1498 (with details of sun and moon 'wrongly' orientated).

93. Henri met de Bles, *The Fall, c.* 1530,
Mauritshuis, The Hague. (See colour details
at figures 96 and 97)

93

Adamites is, of course, derived mainly from records of their calumnators, but it is possible to conjecture that by their ritual nakedness, involving worship and fellowship in underground places reminiscent of the ancient mysteries, they were seeking to attain a state of paradisical innocence. Fraenger,[12] in following such conjectures, admits that the reports do lead to the impression that the Adamites adopted the apocryphal saying of Jesus, the answer to Salome's question as to when death would have an end and the kingdom of Christ begin: 'When ye tread underfoot the garb of shame, and when the two things are one, and the outer is as the inner, and the male as the female, so that there is neither male nor female. . . I have come to undo the works of woman'.

Since it was widely believed that the Adamites' most striking heretical views were connected with the nature of sex, it was a comparatively easy matter for the Inquisitors to label them with dreadful promiscuities and orgiastic rites which almost certainly they did not practice.[13] In spite of bitter persecution, the Adamites and related sects did not entirely disappear until the first half of the sixteenth century.[14] During the period of their greatest power, such heretical sects were sufficiently well organised into communities to produce works of art in support of their particular beliefs. Naturally, such works of art had to be of an occult kind, involved with a particularly well-hidden or specialised symbolism, for detection by the Inquisition would inevitably lead to condemnation and both the artist and painting could be thrown to the flames.

One or two of such heretical paintings, originally intelligible only to those initiated into the teachings of a particular sect, have in fact survived, and a few details about the artists who worked within or on behalf of such sects have come down to us.[15] One such artist, who lived in the early sixteenth century, is Henri met de Bles, whose paintings reveal occult devices and a secret geometry which make his intentions virtually inaccessible to those without a knowledge of the heretical beliefs of the Adamites with whom he was almost certainly connected.

Unlike the work of his contemporary Bosch, whose enigmatic symbolism immediately suggests an heretical interpretation,[16] the paintings of Bles attract little attention, and little is known about his life.[17] His pictures are worth close examination, however, for they contain signs of a consummate skill in the handling of occult themes.

Bles' finest painting, the roundel called *The Fall* (figure 93) was probably painted for a member of the Adamite

94. Woodcut from T. Norton, *Ordinall of Alchemy,* 1652—the dragons, as lunar nodes, with wrongly orientated sun and moon. (Below, detail from *The Fall,* with wrongly orientated moon)

94

Ever kepe thow man both nyght and day,
Of thy desyres thow mayst not mysse,
And alleso of heven that swetz blesse.

sect, since the imagery contained within its secret geometry is in effect a homily on the nature of man's sexuality. It is especially interesting in our present context, not merely because it is an occult painting, but also because it is rooted in the solar-lunar imagery which permeates esoteric symbolism.

The roundel was painted at the beginning of the sixteenth century, and superficially appears as an ordinary, if beautiful, illustration of the four main stages in the *Genesis* story of the Creation and Fall. The four incidents are depicted in continuous representation, which is to say that events quite separate in time are painted as occurring contemporaneously within the single landscape.

To the right of the central fountain of life, God is addressing Adam and Eve (figure 96). Below this group, He is creating Eve from the rib of the sleeping Adam, and her head is already formed at the end of the bone. Towards the left of the fountain, Eve is being tempted by the serpent curled around the tree (figure 97), whilst to the extreme left the Seraph drives the unfortunate naked couple from the Garden. Around the feet of the various groups are a number of animals. The most important of these are the curious leviathan, a rabbit, a stag, a cock, a lion, a monkey, a goat, a dog and a hog.

The first key to the occult significance of this painting actually lies outside the action of the picture itself, on the painted periphery which represents the heavens, or the spiritual world around the Garden of Eden. On this painted band are several fixed stars, a few birds and the Sun and Moon: these luminaries are painted on opposite sides of the picture, which means that they are 'in opposition'. The Moon is full, but Henri Bles has followed the occult tradition, and has painted it as a crescent, with the arc pointing away from the sun. This imagery is probably derived from the occult view of the eternal warfare between the lunar and solar spirits, which permeates alchemical illustrations as a recurrent theme (figure 94).

In the roundel this crescent moon is nearer to the central circle of the picture than the sun, which might lead one to suspect that Bles is interested in the influence which the baleful moon exercises over the Garden of Eden.

For all its superficial appearance, the outer concentric band which contains the luminaries is not intended to depict the skies above Eden, which are in any case clearly visible above the mountains in the background: it is intended to represent two of the four elements of the ancients—those of Air and Fire. The fact that this band is

95. *The Creation of Eve,* frontispiece woodcut to the 15th century Kolner Bible.

96

96. Detail from Henri met de Bles, *The Fall, c.* 1530. Mauritshuis, The Hague. The warning in the Garden, and the creation of Eve.

97. Detail of *The Fall*—the Temptation, and the Expulsion.

97

populated with birds and studded with stars (and of course with the luminaries) suggests both the idea of the physical Air in which the birds fly, and the Fire of which the stars were supposed to consist. In the ancient Ptolemaic view of the world, Air and Fire were the two elements which seek to rise upwards, to expand out into the cosmos away from the cold earth, to their 'proper sphere' which was indeed believed to be precisely two spheres enclosing the earth (figure 95).[18]

The elements of Earth and Water have been painted on the inner part of the panel, for the Patinir-like mountains symbolize the heavy earth, and the sea and rivers symbolize the waters. These are the two elements which strive towards the centre of the earth, and are therefore appropriately placed in the centre of the roundel.

Thus, Henri Bles has painted the four elements in their rightful place—Fire and Air above, Earth and Water below, suggestive of a spiritual harmony which prefigures the harmony of the Garden itself. A related schema of this harmony is to be found in the title page of the fifteenth century Kolner bible (figure 95) in which the creation of Eve in the Garden of Eden is contained embryo-like in a series of concentric devices. The outer circle shows the celestial hierarchies, whilst the next contains the mediaeval symbol for clouds (the undulating band) which represent Air, and the stars, which symbolize Fire. The next band is infested with fish, and clearly this represents Water. The roundel of Eden is mountainous enough to suggest the idea of weighty Earth. Between the Air and Water bands is found a crescent moon and sun: once more the crescent of the moon is pointing away from the solar orb in an unnatural orientation.

In the Bles' roundel, the inclination of the Sun-Moon axis has been carefully arranged, so that the 'action' of the human and celestial figures is contained within an arc of the roundel itself, with one crescent tip the 'creation of Eve', the other crescent tip the 'expulsion'. As befits the title of the picture, the centre of this crescent, exactly between the Sun-Moon axis, shows Eve taking the fruit from the forbidden tree. This crescent form was obviously intended to echo the crescent form of the moon on the outer periphery of the roundel, and to suggest therefore a link between the Genesis story and the moon.

Two important details have in fact been excluded from this lunar crescent: the fountain of life, which is to the centre of the roundel, and the group which consists of God talking to Adam and Eve. Since at this stage of the creation

98. Detail from Hieronymus Bosch, *The Temptation of Saint Anthony,* inner panel, *c.*1505? Museu Nacional de Arte Antiga, Lisbon.

99. Two details from *The Fall* (figure 93) to show the 'wrongly' orientated moon across the diameter of the roundel.

99

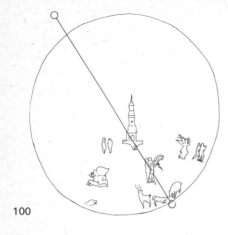

100

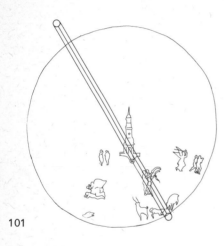

101

102

story Adam and Eve are still uncontaminated by the lunar forces, they are excluded from the influence of the lunar crescent.

This curious—almost hermaphrodite—group of Adam and Eve indicates a point at which Bles has departed from official Christian dogma in this painting. From the attitude of this 'pair', and from the gesture of God who appears to be warning them, one must assume that God is telling Adam and Eve not to eat of the fruit of the tree of good and evil. However, in terms of biblical sequence, God told man not to eat of the tree *before* he created Eve.[19] Henri Bles probably had in mind the frequently overlooked text in Genesis which refers to the creation of a male-female hermaphrodite long before the creation of Adam:

> And God created man in his own image; in the image of God created he him; male and female created he them.[20]

In this same biblical account, it is only after the 'seventh day', that man is created:

> And the Lord God formed man of the dust of the earth, and breathed into his face the breath of life; and man was made into a living soul.[21]

The manner in which these two passages contradict the conventional view of the creation story has fascinated many occultists,[22] and it is quite conceivable that the Adamites themselves were aware of the implications of this 'duality' of creation—especially since, later in the biblical narrative, Eve is created as a separate being from the rib of Adam. It is very likely the connection between this painting and the Adamite sect which has led to the most important single *Genesis* story, the creation of Adam, being left out entirely from the pictorial narrative. The major theme of the roundel is the sexual implications underlying the solar-lunar forces: it is therefore almost inevitable that Bles should concentrate on the dual male-female relations, rather than with the account of one individual.

If a line is drawn from the centre of the sun, at the top of the roundel, exactly to the centre of the lunar crescent, then this line passes exactly through the sexual organs of Adam (figure 100). This is a secret way of indicating the occult truth that the struggle between the solar and lunar forces is most intense at man's generative organs. It is through sex that man is most open to both temptation and spiritual development. This links with the expressed aim of the Adamites, which was to

purify the physiological aspect of procreation to such an

extent that it should no longer be felt as a humiliating animal act, but as the expression of an exalting, divine, creative purification.[23]

Such an admission clearly refers to two quite different types of sex—the 'natural' and the 'spiritual'. This dual approach is emphasised within the roundel by a most remarkable geometric device, both linked with the tangential lines connecting the Sun and Moon (figure 101). One of these lines passes through the central hole of the pipe from which flows the waters of life into Eden, with the intention of showing that the solar aspect of the sexual act is linked with the divine in man. This central point in the roundel is ejecting a kind of solar semen.

A similar tangential line passes through the hand of Eve, reaching out for the fruit. This intersection symbolizes the ultimate downfall of man, his descent into matter, through the temptation of the serpent: from this point in space and time, the 'natural' man is born. The fruit represents the spiritual poison which injects into the world the 'unclean' carnal sex which Mechthild wrote about.

Bles employs an additional secret geometry to reflect upon this dual nature of 'natural' and 'spiritual' sexuality. He takes the solar fount as a fulcrum of balance (figure 102), and places the androgyne group on one side, the expelled couple to the other. It is no accident that the line runs precisely through the sexual parts of the two groups, one innocent, the other guilty.

One would expect a similar balance in the lower lunar world, to reflect the solar balance. At the bottom of the picture, on the periphery of the inner roundel, and just above the lunar crescent are two animals—a dog and a hog (figure 94). These symbolize anger and greed in sixteenth century iconography. Within this context they represent a purely 'lunar' sexuality, which offers neither creativity nor spirituality to develop, for they operate only in the lower part of the 'natural' man. This baleful lower force of the moon finds a striking parallel in the Tarot card called *The Moon* (figure 103), derived from iconography which might well have been originated in heretical groups in the late mediaeval period.[24]

Henri Bles refines this visual doctrine with two further geometric devices. Immediately between the tempted Adam and Eve of the central group and the expulsion group he has painted a pair of copulating sheep (figure 97). He points to the connection between the two groups by making the curious shape of the serpent echo the posture of the copulating animals: the snake has domination over

100. The line joining the sun and moon across the roundel passes through the sexual parts of Adam.

101. The tangential lines from the orbs of the sun and moon pass through the fountain source and the fruit.

102. A line joining the sexual parts of the two groups of Adam and Eve passes through the fountain source: the line joining the sexual parts of the expelled couple and the leviathan passes through a pair of copulating sheep. (See colour plate 97)

103. The 'Moon' card of the Tarot pack.

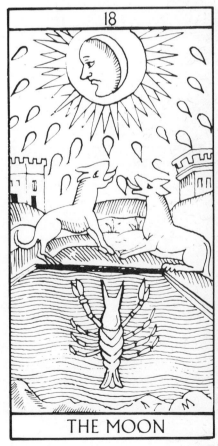

the copulating sheep, in much the same way that it now has domination over the expelled couple. Man, the sheep whom Christ would wish to save, occupies himself in mere fornication, in expression of his lunar 'natural' lusts!

A more refined geometric device employed by Bles introduces a circular construction upon which the harmony of the picture largely depends. If a centre is located upon the important sun-moon axis, just below the water source (figure 104), a circle may be traced which passes through several important pictorial elements, thereby secretly binding them together. To the left of the picture it passes through the hand of the Seraph wielding his sword, then through the mouths of the two animals in conflict at the base of the roundel, and then through the hand of God, holding Adam's rib. As a geometric device, it suggests a relationship between the bone (or rib) and the sword, as well as linking these with the lunar forces of the two animals below. The bone is being used to alleviate Adam's loneliness, to extend harmony into the garden, whilst the sword is being used to expel man from the harmonic conditions of the garden. Two extremes are represented in this geometry.

Both the sword and the bone are important symbols in this picture. An understanding of this symbolism leads us into the domain of astrology, where the planet Mars has a dual role, being associated both with the creative activity and with the repr sive side of man. Many relevant associations drawn by occultists with the planet Mars may be seen in the woodcut by Beham at figure 105, intended to show the occupations of the children of Mars. We see violence, repression, sexual assault, and, in the heavens, the warlike Mars being driven by a pair of dogs. The dual, almost contradictory, roles of Mars are expressed in the double rulership he holds over the zodiacal signs Aries and Scorpio, the symbols for which are blazoned on his wheels.

Creative, or *positive* Mars, as the astrologers term it, rules the zodiacal sign Aries. This is the sign which rules over the head in the human frame (figure 61), and is associated with creative thinking. It is this connection with the head which explains why Henri Bles has shown the rib in the creative hand of God as already formed into the *head* of Eve. This rib represents the creative instrument of the Mars impulse.

The *negative* side of Mars has rulership over the zodiacal sign Scorpio,[25] and is associated with the sexual parts of the human anatomy, with the 'secrets', as the mediaeval

104. Two concentric circles within the secret geometry, the inner linking the sword with the rib of Adam; the outer linking the sexual parts of the couple with the moon and the leviathan.

105. Sebald Beham, *The Children of Mars*, woodcut of *c*. 1530.

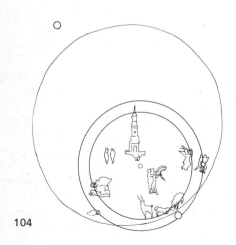

104

106. The chariot of Mars, early 15th century fresco in the Civil Offices, Siena.

106

astrologers often called them (figure 61). The zodiacal Scorpio has held a rather unfortunate association in astrology, and in consequence it has been linked with violence, rapine, sexual license, and with death itself—even with the purgatorial punishments meted out after death. This explains why Bles has chosen a sword as a symbol of the other polarity of Mars.

On the one side, then, is the spiritualised, creative human energy, linked with the sexual parts, and on the other side, the aggressive brutalised repressive energy, linked with the sexual parts. The common element is Mars, and we might therefore expect to find a Martian connection in the third nodal point of this circle of figure 104. In fact, the dog itself is one of the attributes of Mars. The chariot of figure 105 is drawn by dogs; a more beautiful example is found in the fourteenth century personification of Mars the warrior on an arch in the Civil Offices at Siena (figure 106). Bles would have little hesitation in adopting it as a symbol of degenerate or violent sexuality, which is one of the characteristics of negative Mars.

The secret geometry of the circle in figure 104 sets out a clear message to those who can follow its hidden connections. It insists that there are two outlets for sexuality—one is creative, and linked with God, the other is violent and linked with the fallen man. The creative outlet is the bringer of life to another human being, whilst the destructive outlet is selfish, and leads to alienation, symbolized here as the expulsion from the garden. These two extremes are conjoined at a purely animal level, and fall entirely under the dominion of the moon, where the creative energies are transformed into violence and greed.

In order to reveal the sexual condition of the expelled couple—that is, all human beings who dwell outside of grace, so far as the Adamites are concerned—Bles has added an outer concentric circle to this secret geometry (figure 104). The moon itself marks the lowest point of the circumference of this circle, which also embraces the sexual parts of the expelled couple, and the mouth of the sea monster, below the group depicting the creation of Eve. Once again, the occult message is revealed in the secret geometry: since this outer circle contains no contact with the spiritual world, it may have reference only to man's state of alienation from the Godhead. Once outside Eden, out of touch with his true spiritual being, man's sexual desires are held under the control of the leviathan monster and the moon. He is in a sense a sexual lunatic!

The head of the leviathan below the creative group (figure 96) is a symbol of the level to which the creative Arietan head of Eve may degenerate to, when spirituality is abandoned.

As though to remove any doubts as to the implications of this outer circle, Bles has established another connection, though this time a linear one (figure 102). This passes through the sexual parts of the expelled couple, directly through the sexual parts of the copulating sheep, and in to the head of the leviathan. The connection is a further commentary in secret geometry on man's dependence upon the lunar forces.

The secret geometry which speaks so compellingly about the division in man after the fall from grace is paralleled in the symbolism of the animals gathered in this Paradise. The casual observer may not be blamed for assuming that Bles has painted his groups of animals in the foreground (figure 97) merely to point to another stage of the *Genesis* account of creation, and to suggest the harmony which reigned in the Garden. After all, here one finds the lion is lying down with the stag and rabbit, and save for the barking of the dog, a general harmony and calm is expressed in the scene. However, in keeping with the mediaeval tradition within which he worked, Bles has chosen to group the animals together in a symbolic manner. In keeping with occult belief, the animals symbolize on one level the vestigial remains of forces which are still to be found in a less powerful state in all humans: these animals symbolize the unredeemed elements in man.[26]

There are two main groups of animals. There are four animals to the left of the goat, and the dog-hog group to his right. This grouping is by no means accidental.

The four couchant animals represent the four humours of the alchemists and astrologers, the human expression of the four elements. The lion symbolizes the *choleric* type, the expression of Fire, seen to the right of the choleric figure in a sixteenth century Shepherd's Calendar (figure 107), who is standing on flames, with a drawn sword, illustrative of the fact that the choleric is easily moved to anger. This lion has his back to the rabbit which is symbolic of the *phlegmatic* type, the expression of Water. The rabbit appears as a symbol of the phlegmatic in the famous engraving by Durer of *Adam and Eve*. The monkey represents the *sanguine* type, the expression of the element of Air, also in this role in figure 107, with the human figure standing upon 'Air' clouds, holding a bird in

107. 15th century woodcut of the choleric temperament, with attendant lion and the sanguine temperament, with attendant monkey.

107

108

his left hand. The stag, which appears also in the Durer print (figure 108) represents the *melancholic* type, the expression of the Earth element in man.

These four couchant animals are intended to point to the occult tradition that before the fall of man, the four elements were perfectly balanced within the body of Adam. Because things were so harmonized in this balance, there could be no illness, since illness was merely an excess of deficiency in one or more of the humours within the body.[27] This tradition explains why the animals are at rest, couchant.

However, this four-fold harmony with the garden is to be disrupted, for once the fruit has been eaten, the four elements will be in discord, and Adam's descendants will be subject to disturbing passions. As symbol of this awakening chaos, Henri Bles has placed a cock above the group (figure 97). Within the popular symbolism of his time, it was held that the lion, that symbol for courage and physical strength, actually feared the cock![28] Thus, with the Fall, and with the discord of the pact between the four elements, Leo the lion, who has rule over the human heart (figure 61), is disturbed into fear, which until this time has been stranger to the garden.

The group behind the dividing goat shows that the discord has already broken out: the dog snarls at the hog, and the dominion of the lunar forces begins. The connection between the aggression of the dog and the Mars force has been explored: the hog also represents a low-grade human propensity, that of sensuality and greed. The pig or hog is one of the attributes of Anthony Abbot, simply because the Saint is supposed to have vanquished from his person the demons of sensuality and gluttony.

On the one side is the pact of the four elements: on the other side, the open discord between the lunar forces. Standing between them is the goat himself, an image so closely associated with the Devil that it has become a general part of popular folklore that he is president over the orgiastic rituals of witchcraft in the form of a goat.

The fact is that the roundel, in both its secret geometry and in its animal symbolism, presents an occult view of sex which would be regarded as heretical by the mediaeval Church.[29] Whilst Bles points to the obvious lunar influence, and indicates man's dependence upon lower drives in the sexual nature (as does, indeed, the orthodox religious view), he points also to the possibility of a different kind of sexuality, or use of sexual energies. The message of the picture proclaims that the divine nature of sex is being misused when it is indulged purely for the sake of pleasure: such misuses carry the human to a bestial condition, which in turn demotes the soul to the lunar world of Purgatory.

Since this view corresponds to the attitudes concerning the sexual nature of man put forward by the Adamites, it is safe to assume that Henri Bles was either himself a member of this group, or was commissioned to paint the roundel for them, replete with its wealth of secret geometry and symbolism. Indeed, it could be that Bles was among the last numbers of the surviving school of heretical painters, the major works of which were either destroyed by the Inquisition, or which still remain 'lost' to us precisely because they were painted with secret geometries which have not yet been revealed.

Whilst it is tempting to see Bles' roundel as a beautiful picture of an orthodox theme—and thus miss the esoteric meaning—it is just not possible to regard the works of Hieronymus Bosch as anything other than occult. The result is that Bosch has been approached by a number of occultists and art historians who have erected around him a whole battery of hypotheses, all of which mask the fact that whilst virtually nothing is known about Bosch the man, even less is known about his work, his symbolism and the esoteric school for which he undoubtedly worked.

The theories abound. His subject is Hell,[30] he is the 'demon maker',[31] he depicts 'terrible dreamlike fantasies', even though these are still 'divine'.[32] Bosch is accused of religious heresy in the twentieth century,[33] but in the sixteenth century, when there was probably less heresy, but when it was more easily recognised, he was cleared of such a charge.[34] He is explained in terms of the alchemical tradition,[35] the Rosicrucian tradition,[36] by certain astrological conventions[37] (themselves misunderstood and inaccurately reported); he is explained by the 'unconscious', in modern psychoanalytical terms linked with dream structures,[38] and by the 'conscious', in his systematic use of metaphorical figures of speech:[39] indeed, as Friedlander points out, there is 'no painter who has baffled, and even defeated, the historian to the same extent as Hieronymus Bosch'.[40] The very diversity of such hypotheses indicates that Bosch is difficult of interpretation, an outsider to conventional art-historical methods.

A superficial glance at the images such as those in figure 109 might explain why Bosch is so frequently regarded as a 'demon maker'. A deeper study of such images,

108. Detail from Durer's *Adam and Eve*, engraving of 1503.

109. Detail from the left-hand wing of Hieronymus Bosch, *The Garden of Earthly Delights,* early 16th century. Prado, Madrid.

109

110. Syncretic zodiac, from Kircher, *Oedipus Aegyptiacus,* 1653. The detail shows *Ichton,* from the Pisces segment.

111. Detail of Hieronymus Bosch, *The Temptation of Saint Anthony,* inner panel, *c.* 1505? Museu Nacional de Arte Antiga, Lisbon. (See colour plate 98)

110

however, reveals Bosch to be more deeply involved with occultism than a mere demon maker would be, and the marked contrast between the superficial interpretation and the deeper occult would indicate that there is a message in the work of Bosch which has so far evaded interpretation. The contrast is therefore worth examining.

The detail at figure 98 is taken from a theme derived from the demonological strains in the popular *Legenda Aurea* of Vorggine.[41] The detail has been explained in terms of the 'demon maker' by Friedlander, who has traced in Bosch the habit of giving birth to monsters, of confusing God's world by turning it inside out: he pictures the detail of the curious rider as 'an old hag, holding an infant in her arms, riding on a beast that is half pig and half hare. Her lower half is a fish-tail, her head-gear a hollow log'.[42] If the detail is to be understood in such a way, then it is indeed difficult to see it as anything other than a 'birth of monsters', a hybrid of siren or mermaid grown old. However, Friedlander's interpretation prevents him from linking the rider with an old iconographic tradition, probably the one which Bosch had in mind. For in fact this is not the face of an old hag, but of a man; and the beast he rides is neither half pig nor half hare, but a rat.

A familiarity with occult concepts would enable one to interpret this detail as a complex, though superbly constructed, diatribe against the decadent Church Triumphant, the most constant theme of heretics and would-be heretics in the mediaeval era. The significance of the child in the branch-like grasp of this humanoid is lost, unless one is able to relate the whole figure of the rider to the Babylonian *Oannes,* himself linked with Christ,[43] and to the *Ichton*[44] derived from this Babylonian image, and preserved in the esoteric zodiac under that name, though linked with Pisces (figure 110).[45] In this image Ichton is a fish-tailed man holding in one hand a masonic rule, and in the other a child.

The meaning of the Piscean imagery within the Christian hermetic tradition has been sufficiently discussed for the importance of this link with Pisces—the fish and the Child—to be grasped, but other important occult implications are contained within this heretical image by virtue of its connection with Oannes, who was credited with the creation of man from clay—which explains why the figure of Ichton in figure 110 is holding a baby (or small man) in his hand. Within this framework, the child in the hands of Bosch's tree-man-fish is at once Jesus and Adam, a graphic idea which no doubt links with the habit

of the early Church fathers of calling Christ the 'second Adam'. There could be few more subtle ways of combining images so potent within Christianity in order to mock the Church Triumphant, for not only are there undertones of Adam and Christ, but also explicit references to the swaddling clothes of the Luke Jesus, and to the image of the Virgin Mary holding the child.

Now, given sufficient erudition in esoteric and occult texts, it is a relatively easy matter to construct explanations for the individual symbols within the work of Bosch, in much the same spirit as we have explained the tree-man-fish. Such a level of interpretation naturally assists in deepening one's awareness of the occult strains in Bosch's work: for example, we may be able to recognize through this Adamic-Christian imagery the import of the dead tree headgear worn by *Ichton*, for this tree is at once the tree of Adam—the withered tree of Paradise which brought death into the world—and the tree upon which the World Saviour was hanged, to conquer death. Yet, our understanding of such symbols must remain decidedly incomplete until we can link them together within the picture as a unity, and resolve the meaning of the picture as a whole. We must for example be in a position to understand why the figure is sitting on the back of a rat, why there is a curious grisaille rider behind the rat, why this curious man-fish is sitting on a red mantle, and why this mockery of the Piscean Church Triumphant is attacking St. Anthony at all. In effect, we must realise that what is important about the occult strains in Bosch is not merely the individual symbols, which may be more or less interpreted according to one's knowledge of mediaeval occult lore, but the *underlying philosophical unity*, the key to which in every single case is missing. Even a brief survey of this symbolism, lost as it is in an arid desert of our ignorance concerning Bosch's actual intentions, explains why the paintings have become happy hunting grounds for occultists and historians alike.

Among the more inspired and reliable theories concerning the occult unity underlying Bosch's work is that developed by Fraenger,[46] which traces within his imagery certain heretical strains which were specifically connected with the Adamites. Such a connection has of course already been suggested between the Adamites and Bles, through analysis of the secret geometry underlying a single roundel. In fact, a secret geometry similar to that used by Bles, meaningfully linked with the sexual parts of the human figure, is found also in the work of Bosch, and

112. The right-hand wing of Hieronymus Bosch, *The Garden of Earthly Delights,* early 16th century. Prado, Madrid. (See colour plates 121 and 122)

112

may also suggest a connection with the sexual heresies of the Adamites. This may be seen as supporting Fraenger's general hypotheses, for whilst this historian has concentrated his argument on the literary and visual themes within Bosch's paintings, it is quite possible to approach the subject from another angle, and to indicate a secret geometry directly linked with sexual themes reminiscent of the Adamite heresies, and steeped in esoteric lore.

An example of this secret geometry may be seen in the right hand wing of the triptych of the so-called *Garden of Earthly Delights*—a picture which has little to do with the Earth, and even less with delights (figure 112). If the hole at the centre of the fountain is used as a fulcrum, two lines may be drawn through its centre to link the sexual parts of the couple with the sexual symbols at the top of the panel (figure 113). The line commencing at Eve's pudenda terminates in a hole in the left-hand rocks, through which a serpentine line of birds is flying (figure 122). The line commencing at Adam's penis terminates in a curious spindle and ball which on analysis proves to be both creative and sexual. Whilst the imagery evoked by this secret geometry is in some respects a little more elusive than that used by Bles, we may none the less discern a similar use of solar-lunar contrasts, as in the Bles roundel.

On the earth plane, the original couple are in the presence of Christ. It seems that Adam has just awakened from a deep sleep and is being presented to Eve. The physical forms of the couple are so related as to indicate a potential physical conjunction: the concave curve of Adam's body forms a matrix to the convex form of Eve—postures redolent of sexual implication which is seen in the alert glance of Adam, and in the demure gesture of Eve. Within strictly theological contexts, this group within the garden is heretical, for it depicts Christ, rather than God, as the creator of Eve, but in terms of the Adamite theme, it is Christ who brings together human beings. The occult link between Adam and Christ is pointed out in the astrological Piscean device which places the feet of Adam over the feet of Christ. This Piscean gesture is perhaps intended to harmonise with the imagery within the rest of the panel, which is directly linked with one of the other Water signs of the zodiac, Cancer.

It has been remarked that the fountain in the centre of this innocent garden is cancroid in shape and colour, and 'resembles the shell of a crab standing upright, crowned with a half moon with the pincers raised'.[47] Whilst this might be a somewhat imaginative interpretation of the

113. Structural relationship between the sexual parts of Adam and Eve and the sexual symbols in the upper part of the panel: the lines meet at the central hole of the fountain.

113

form of this fountain, there is no doubt that certain elements within its construction are cancroid: the colour is that of boiled crab, whilst the articulation of forms, and many of the textures, remind one of the crab's shell. The spiked lunar crescent almost at the top of the fountain appears to confirm the connection between this structure and the sign of the Crab, which is ruled by the planet Moon (figure 114).

The iconographic link between the fountain and the sign Cancer is by no means accidental, for it introduces certain occult themes connected with the idea of the Creation of the World. Through this cancroid fountain Bosch is pointing to a widely spread astrological tradition which maintains that the birth of the World (and indeed the birth of Adam and Eve) took place under zodiacal Cancer. Several *Themae Mundi*—'horoscopes for the birth of the world'—were in common currency in mediaeval times,[48] and in all the ancient examples, the birth of the earth is shown to have taken place when Cancer was on the Ascendant (that is, on the Eastern horizon), in some examples with the Moon itself in this same watery sign.

The cancroid and lunar forms of the fountain link with the theme of Creation which permeates the whole painting, whilst the location of the fountain, immediately above the head of Christ, who is reconciling the couple, is itself intended to remind one of the ecclesiastical view, expressed by Saint Ambrose, that Christ was 'the fountain which irrigated Paradise'.[49] Just as the couple are united by the body of Christ below, so are the solar and lunar forces, linked with the separate sexual spheres, united in the body of Christ, in their conjuncting lines at the centre of the fountain. This fountain is, then, at once Cancerian and Piscean because of the Sun-God Christ. Bosch's combination of solar and lunar imagery is breathtaking in its heretical and Christian implications.

In the top of the panel (figure 122) there is a 'celestial' statement of the male-female imagery in the Adam and Eve below, expressed in the two groups of rocks. These curious rocks abound in solar-lunar imagery, but if we restrict our examination exclusively to the terminal points of the secret geometry (figure 113), we shall find further evidence in support of the claim that Bosch's art was linked with the Adamite heresy.

The line connecting with Eve's private parts terminates in the womb-like circle through which flies a serpentine line of swallows. The mediaeval bestiaries taught that the swallow hibernated in mud during the winter, and its

114. 15th century woodcut of Mercury and Moon. The crescent Moon is placed over the sexual parts of the female; the sign Cancer, ruled by the moon, is partly visible.

114

advent in the spring was looked upon as a rebirth from the death state of winter. For this reason, the bird was taken as a symbol of birth, especially of the Incarnation of Christ.[50] Amidst these rocks a creature linked with the Christ is being *born* from this hole, which is itself linked with the sexual parts of Eve. This is a striking image which portrays birth of a celestial order, linked with the female Moon. We might reasonably expect similar sexual symbolism, linked with the male Sun, on the opposite side of the panel.

The line proceeding from the sexual parts of Adam (figure 113) terminates in the curious spindle and ball, which dangles from the sharp protruberance of the blue rock (figure 121). The very fact that a crescent moon dangles to the left of this, over a cluster of trees, might suggest that this penis-like form is intended to be a sun-symbol of some kind. The fact is, however, that this form is precisely one of the most common mediaeval sigils for the Sun itself, which was commonly presented in a penis-like form. The example from a Dutch alchemical manuscript, written contemporaneously with Bosch (figure 115), gives two variants, though sigils precisely in the form painted by Bosch may be found in other alchemical documents.[51] The symbol is at once solar, sexual, and whilst linked with Adam, is also, through the solar overtones, linked with Christ.

The noticeable reversal of the common lunar-solar imagery and the traditional colours results from the secret geometry, since the intersection of the Adam and Eve imagery at the central fulcrum of the fountain necessitates that the imagery which associates Eve with the lunar left, Adam with the solar right, should be reversed. The feminine fecund womb is of necessity to the right, but becomes creative by virtue of the warm (masculine) colours; whilst the male penis is of necessity to the left, but passive by virtue of the cold blue colours. There is a mixing of male and female, solar and lunar, imagery by virtue of the intercession of the Christ fountain. In many respects, this is a brilliant visual expression of the Adamite belief that the merging of male and female on the physical plane might lead one to Christ, might indeed be practised in such a way as to become a prayer in the sight of God.

Such analyses, whilst supporting the general argument for 'heresy', indicate that Bosch's prolix imagery encourages arcane speculation, virtually demands an unrestrained iconographic esotericism. This might reasonably suggest that even those of his pictures which do not appear to demand an interpretation within the framework of

115. Sixteenth century alchemical manuscript from Leiden University Library: three of the mediaeval sigils for the sun are on the fourth line from the bottom.

116. Hieronymus Bosch, *Christ Crowned with Thorns,* early 16th century. National Gallery, London.

115

116

117

118

119

120

occult ideas, may however be rooted in arcane symbolism, itself 'natural' to the mediaeval mind, yet far removed from the modern. This does in fact prove to be the case.

By way of example, we may take the painting *Christ Crowned with Thorns* (figure 116). From an occult point of view, the most obvious theme within this picture is the connection between the four faces of the tormentors, and the four temperaments, derived from the late mediaeval doctrine concerning the way in which the four elements manifest through the microcosm.[52] This mediaeval tradition links the element of Fire with the *Choleric* temperament, Air with the *Sanguine*, Water with the *Phlegmatic*, and Earth with the *Melancholic*.

The popular descriptions and woodcuts which portrayed the four temperaments, and which promulgated the theories of the physiognomic types, had a profound influence on the so-called 'realism' of late mediaeval and Renaissance art, [53] and there is much evidence that Bosch himself was influenced by such occult streams. In this picture, for example, the profile of the tormentor in the bottom left—who proves on analysis to be the representative of the Phlegmatic type, is related to the stock figure linked with the description of a physiognomy believed to be that of Judas Iscariot, who in the popular astrological tradition is associated with the water sign Scorpio (figure 119):

> for indeed the eyes are sharp, the nose aquiline, though terminating in a point, and the lips are thin, drawn inwards towards the gums; such (forms) indicate a man given to treachery.[54]

This description must be related to the tradition within the same doctrine of physiognomy that a man with a poor or straggling beard is sure to be lacking in virility[55]—a fairly heavy charge in mediaeval life.

In both religious and secular imagery it was common enough to find portrayals of Christ, and of such personifications as *Philosophia,* surrounded by the four elements, either in a schematic presentation of the elements themselves (figure 124), or in an image where He is depicted surrounded by the four temperaments (figure 125). A related secular image by Durer exists in which the female personification *Philosophia* is surrounded by the four temperamental types (figure 127) as well as by the four philosophical types of humanity, the four winds, and so on. In the arrangement of figure 127 the compositional device of the floral vesica reminds one of the image of the *anima mundi* of the Tarot Card (figure 129), which has

117–120. Details from figure 116: the four temperamental types, in descending order, the *Choleric*, the *Sanguine*, the *Phlegmatic* and the *Melancholic*.

121. The right-hand wing of Hieronymus Bosch, *The Garden of Earthly Delights*, early 16th century. Prado, Madrid.

122. Detail of figure 121, to show the fountain's cancroid form, and the solar symbol at top left.

121

122

123. Tintoretto, *The Origin of the Milky Way,*
c. 1578. National Gallery, London.

123

gathered in the four corners the four fixed signs of the zodiac, themselves representatives of the four elements.

It is clear from such examples that, in portraying Christ surrounded by his four tormentors, Bosch is working within an established occult imagery in order to suggest that these mockers represent the four cosmic human types. By linking the microcosmic aspects of the four elements with the Christ, Bosch is actually carrying this mockery out of the merely personal into the universal: the Redeemer is being maltreated by all mankind.

The arrangement of the figures, and the symbols invested in their forms and clothing, carry this occult level into more significant realms. In the schematic presentation of the spheres common in mediaeval times, the order of the elements (in descent from the Macrocosm) was Fire, Air, Water and Earth. This is exactly the arrangement of the figures in Bosch's picture, and to leave no doubt of his intention, Bosch has presented each of the types in such a way as to allow them to be identified by means of the significance of the special relationship they hold towards Christ, which reveals a particular temperament.

The Fire type—the choleric (figure 117)—is at the top of the picture. His armoured hand signifies the violence associated with the type, a violence so well known that the stereotyped image of the choleric in mediaeval popular broadsheets was that of a man beating a woman (figure 126). The metal fist is more than merely a symbol of repression and dehumanisation, since in the astrological tradition iron is the metal of Mars, the planet which rules over zodiacal Aries, which in turn rules the head of zodiacal man (figure 61). This explains why the choleric is doing the act of violence with a mailed fist, and why he is the one to force the thorns upon Christ's head.

The Air type—the sanguine (figure 118)—is next in descending order: he is resting his hand on the shoulder of Christ, a gesture which has at least a double symbolic implication. First, this gesture reminds one of the idea of intimate and personal speech—it is as though this sanguine type is establishing a relationship with Christ by personal contact, perhaps even being on the point of speaking to Him. Now, it is precisely through the medium of Air that speech is made possible, and for this reason the sanguine type is associated with all modes of speech, from the high drama of acting to meaningless monkey chatter. Just as the choleric expresses his relation to Christ through the 'fire' deed of violence (figure 126), so the sanguine expresses himself through the 'air' deed of communication.

124. 15th century woodcut—Christ standing in the midst of the schematic presentations of the four elements.

125. Christ surrounded by the personifications of the four temperamental types. From the 16th century *Guildbook of the Barber Surgeons of York.* British Museum, London.

124

125

126. The Choleric beating a woman in the passion of anger: from a woodcut in the *Augsburg Calendar,* late 15th century.

127. Albrecht Durer, *Philosophia* surrounded by the four temperaments and the four winds. Woodcut of *c.* 1500.

128. Hieronymus Bosch, *Christ Crowned with Thorns,* early 16th century. National Gallery, London.

126

C Colericus

127

Secondly, in astrology the shoulders and arms of the human body are ruled by the air sign Gemini (figure 61), which perhaps explains the shoulder gesture more fully, and certainly explains the gesture which the sanguine tormentor is making towards the arm of Christ, a gesture rendered more poignant by the fact that his hand holds a stick, symbolic of the cross to which Christ's arms will be nailed later in the day. The oak leaves and acorn in the hat of the sanguine is perhaps derived from the same tradition which encouraged Durer to depict vegetation emerging from the mouth of the sanguine Zephyrus in figure 127—though once again the symbolism is double, for the oak is linked in mediaeval lore with the Cross, this being one of the trees from which it was supposed to have been made. Within this symbolism, the sanguine element is particularly fitting as a link, for it is Christ himself who will be the fruit of the oak cross (the acorn), when He is thrust into the air in order to redeem mankind.

The Water type—the phlegmatic (figure 119)—is the next head in descending order. In this case, his lewd gesture, his hand over Christ's hands, which are in turn located at his private parts, is intended to link with the zodiacal sign Scorpio, the water sign which rules over the private parts of zodiacal man (figure 61). It is of further significance that the Moon, one of the symbols emblazoned on the lower part of his headgear, is associated in the occult tradition, exoterically with the sexual parts, and esoterically with the lunar demons, for whom sexuality is a higher state of awareness, and through which the demons have direct access to man. The gesture of the Water type is virtually such a demonic gesture, reaching towards the seat of man's weakest point. The physiognomical relationship between the phlegmatic and the Scorpionic nature has already been mentioned.

The Earth type—the melancholic (figure 120)—is placed uncomfortably low down in the picture, as befits the position of earth in the scale of being. He is, however, reaching up into the centre of the picture (for this entire pictorial theme is the destruction and torment of the earthly body), and ripping at the garment of Christ—which is to say that by his gesture he is attempting to destroy the physical body of Christ. This symbolism is quite in order, since the Earth element is concerned primarily with the visible physical body of man, as with the physical body of the world. The upward-reaching gesture of the melancholic type is probably intended by Bosch to contrast with the downward motion of the

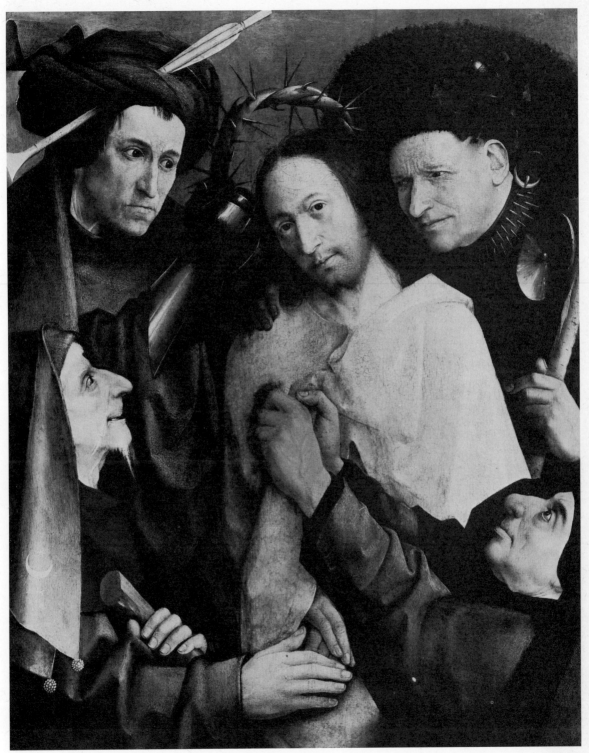

128

129

THE WORLD

130

choleric type, so that the mailed fist may be taken as the potential horizontal bar of a cross, made with the vertical bar of the melancholic gesture. Earth and Fire are depicted in eternal conflict—the Fire nature attacks Christ at the spiritual part, through his head, whilst the Earth nature attacks Him through the lower, physical, parts. A similar potential cross-formation made by the other two is even more obvious, for they both hold wooden staves, virtually at right angles to each other, intended in fact for the flagellation but symbolically for the coming crucifixion.

Thus, the human aspect of Christ is beset by torments at every level of His being, and through each of the four elements. By the Fire element, which works through the spiritual impulse of the Fire sign Aries, he is invested not with the Spirit, as at a baptism, but with the cruel thorns of a martian crown: instead of healing spirit, he is given dead and wounding wood. By the Air type he is being led into a false relationship by a friendly-seeming gesture: the Word is being assailed by the mere word. The Scorpionic gesture of the Water type, with the obscene masturbatory gesture of the left hand, is attacking Christ with the demonic force—the betraying force which is linked with the uterine waters of life, here debased and made rank through a wrong use of sexuality. By the Earth type, the one so concerned with the well-being of the body as to have a reputation for good living, and in extremes for hypochondria, Christ is having his protective sheath, his 'garment', torn away.

In this brilliant image, unique not in its theme, but in its symbolism, we have Christ surrounded by the lower forces of the four elements, reminding one prophetically of the crucifixion. When the deed is done, when Christ is crucified, then indeed Redemption will be a reality, and Christ will have triumphed for ever over the elements. It is for this reason that the four images of the *redeemed* elements—the lion of Fire, the human of Air, the eagle of Water, and the bull of Earth, are placed around the crucified Christ (figure 21), and in the image of *anima* in the Tarot (figure 129). The crucifixion is the high point, the summation of the story of Redemption—the mocking and flagellation of the physical body the low point, a reflection of the debased levels of unredeemed man. Thus, within this image Christ is to be seen as being tormented by those very forces which it is His destiny to redeem. No painting of this subject expresses so well the occult implications, valid at once for the orthodox as for the heretical, as does this remarkable oak panel of Bosch.

One of the last great masters to use mediaeval secret geometric structures was Tintoretto, whose vast workshop in Venice appears to have retained an unusually late contact with earlier traditions. His magnificent canvas *The Origin of the Milky Way* (figure 131) is an excellent example of the survival of this occult imagery, painted at a time when there was a tendency for artists to incorporate hidden structures for purely compositional effects, at the expense of the 'hidden' meanings so beloved by the mediaeval studios.

The composition of *The Origin* is profoundly interesting, for an analysis of its structure reveals it to be twofold. There is a fairly apparent 'aesthetic' structure based on a series of concentric circles, obviously intended to introduce a curvilinear unity into the composition, and there is a second, well hidden 'geometric' structure which is intended to incorporate a hidden meaning well beyond the confines of aesthetic considerations. It is this latter compositional structure which we shall examine here, for it is directly linked with the occult tradition attached to the solar-lunar imagery of occult art, and remains a supreme example of how a great artist may transform a relatively simple—not to say 'overworked'—device, and extend its possibility as a creative force.

Tintoretto's *Origin of the Milky Way* illustrates a legend with which he, or his important patron Tommaso Rangoni,[56] would be familiar through a book on agriculture, known as the *Geoponica*, which had been published in Italian during Tintoretto's youth.[57] The legend tells how Hercules was born of Zeus and the mortal Alcmene. Had the child been fed on the ordinary milk of his mother, then he would himself have become mortal. Zeus naturally wanted his son to be immortal, and therefore pressed his son's face against the nipples of the full breasts of the sleeping goddess Hera. Hercules sucked his fill, and when his lips were removed from the breasts, the milk which squirted into the heavens terminated in stars. This was said to be the origin of our Milky Way.

The masterly composition clearly concerns this part of the myth: Hera has been awakened in surprise at the action of Zeus, and it is this which partly explains her curious posture. The picture deviates to a small extent from the details of the legend, for we see the stars being formed from the streams of milk which are squirted from the breasts under the excess pressure of Hercules. However, there is one most important conclusion in the Byzantine legend which the present composition does not account

129. The 'World' card of the Tarot pack.

130. Christ in Glory, surrounded by the four tetramorphs—detail from the 15th century panel *The Apocalypse* of Master Betram. Victoria and Albert Museum, London.

131. Tintoretto, *The Origin of the Milky Way*, *c*. 1578. National Gallery, London. (See colour plate 123)

131

for. The story tells that the excess milk which dropped on to the surface of the earth was formed into the white lily!

In fact, this part of the story was included on the original painting, which is known to have been on a canvas at least one third larger than the present one. Two drawings of the original composition have survived, one by Jacob Hoefnagel, and the other by Domenico, one of Tintoretto's sons.[58] A reconstruction of the original composition (figure 132) clearly shows the lilies which grew from the spilt milk, and the naked Alcmene, who is reclining on the earth.

This interesting myth concerning the origin of the Milky Way, and the lilies of earth, underlies an occult connection which is drawn between lilies and incarnation—with the concept of 'the descent of spirit into matter'. Just as in the *Primavera* the flowers in the mouth of the nymph Chloris symbolize the descent of the mercurial word, so the white lilies represent the descent of a god, of the Word. This occult link with incarnation perhaps explains why Mary, the mother of Jesus, is generally associated with a lily in the Annunciation scenes (figure 134): the lily is a Christian symbol of 'incarnation', a sign of that miraculous process by which a God becomes man.

Tintoretto obviously reasoned that since the cosmic drama takes place in the spiritual spheres, it would be appropriate for him to base his underlying aesthetic geometry on circles. A concentric arrangement of circles would in any case be a fitting image of the heavens since in his day the geocentric system of spheres had not been displaced by the heliocentric system of Copernicus.[59]

Since the action depicted is creative, involved with both nourishment and birth, it is appropriate that he should choose to locate the centre for this system of concentrics on the sexual parts of Hera. This device is cleverly employed: it is unobtrusive, and *felt* long before it is seen.

The strong curve of the naked Alcmene is clearly intended to unite its rhythm with the strong curvitures of the upper concentrics. She is, however, at the same time cut off from these concentrics, which is the domain not of the human, but of the spiritual. The compositional device is clearly intended to point the moral that earthbeings may well be linked with the gods—may indeed be the prime concern of the gods—yet they do not properly belong to the celestial domain whilst in incarnate form.

In spite of the meaningful manner in which these circles pull the composition into harmony, Tintoretto reserves the real inner content of his *secret* geometry to a second

132. Reconstruction of the original composition of *The Origin of the Milky Way.*

133. Filippo Lippi, *Annunciation, c.* 1450. National Gallery, London.

134. Detail of lilies between the Archangel and the Virgin, from figure 133 above.

132

series of curves and circles, which are imposed upon this 'aesthetic' geometry.

One might imagine that his main compositional problem was that of establishing the centres for a second group of circles—clearly he could not place this centre on the same important point. He located this centre in a very clever way, as the sequences in figure 135 indicate: with two loci at the sexual parts of Hera, and the suckled nipple, he continued a line through these towards the base of the picture, through the lilies, until it cuts the canvas edge. A second line was then drawn from this intersection, horizontally to the picture base, to run through the womb of the reclining nude. A line drawn from this second intersection and taken back through the sexual parts of Hera gives the first centre for the secret circles of this geometry, at the point where it cuts the top of the canvas edge. A compass point on this centre gives a circle which encloses the body and head of Zeus, and even explains the curious form of his movement. It explains also the plunging motion of the putto to his left, which completes the sweep of the circle (figure 136).

When this point is taken as the beginning of another line, extending through the nipple of Hera to cut the canvas edge, a second centre for a circle is obtained. This larger circle passes through the sexual parts of Hera, along the inner edge of her right leg, and embraces the head of the naked Alcmene below.

The visual effect of the two 'secret' circles so obtained is the creation of two spheres which separate the male Zeus from the two females within the picture. The separative force is not quite so strong as this graphic analysis would suggest, however, precisely because the 'aesthetic' geometry of concentrics binds together the god and goddess.

A new (third) centre within the secret geometry is established when a line is drawn from the nipples, back to the lower junction between the horizontal and the frame edge. A third circle drawn from this centre runs through the middle of the second circle, touches the ankle of Hera's right leg, embraces her thigh, head, and at the same time explains the curiously dynamic twist of her body.

The graphic logic underlying this secret geometry (figure 137) is not intended merely as a guide for a complex composition—it is in effect a commentary on the nature of the relationship between Gods and human beings. The fact is that whilst the circle enclosing Zeus is a *solar* symbol—that is, a male god in a circular form—the lower circles, arising from Hera's strange contortion,

133

134

135

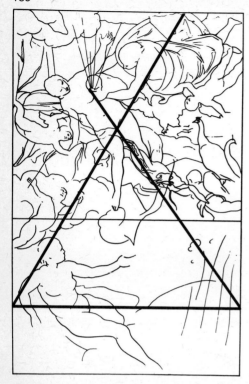

136

produce together the shape of a *lunar* crescent, enfolding a female form.

In this composition the crescent of the 'moon' is correctly orientated to the 'sun': the crescent is bowed out towards the light. This relationship between sun and moon would suggest the idea that there is no warfare, no alienation between the male and female principles, as there is on earth. In spite of the human emotions attributed to the higher gods, by mythmakers, there is no real disharmony or conflict in the celestial spheres. Such discord is possible only on the earth below, where Alcmene rests alone among the lilies of incarnation.

When this lone figure is restored to its rightful place within the composition, the original painting may be seen as a magnificent study of the alienation which the human being experiences from the harmonious spiritual world above. This is surely the secret teaching underlying the Byzantine legend, for it suggests that so alienated is mortal mankind from the world of the immortals, that it is necessary for even a God to resort to trickery in order to permit a mortal child to join his estate.

The myth insists also that what the spiritual beings do in their own sphere profoundly influences the material world. The tricking of Hera, and the theft of her milk, has consequences on a cosmic scale, for it created the eternal stars which keep their ancient places, and the lilies of the field, which are the very symbols of transience.

The profound duality of the compositional method employed by Tintoretto places this canvas astride two worlds. In its insistence upon a series of concentric harmonies, the painting is concerned with the aesthetic structures which will obsess artists in the coming centuries. In its insistence upon a logic of secret geometry, it has clear affinities with the mediaeval workshops.

There was almost a cosmic significance in the mutilation of the original Tintoretto canvas, for when Alcmene and the flowers were severed from the celestial world above, this was virtually a symbolic expression of what has happened to mankind as a whole since the renaissance. Man has himself been severed from the ancient contact with the spiritual world, and the knowledge of the ancient music of the spheres, which was a dance of spirit, between incarnation and excarnation, between the stars and the flowers. *The Origin of the Milky Way* stands astride a bifurcating road: for all its modernity of style and vision, it represents the last flowering of an art rooted in the occult leaf-drift of centuries. ↰

135. Compositional analysis of *The Origin of the Milky Way:* location of the first centre, as explained on page 105.

136. Compositional analysis of *The Origin of the Milky Way:* location of the second centre, as explained on page 105.

137. Compositional analysis of *The Origin of the Milky Way:* location of the third centre, by which the crescent is constructed—see page 105.

137

138

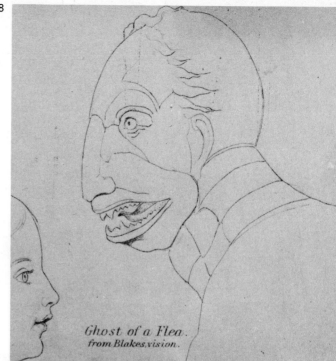

Ghost of a Flea.
from Blakes vision.

138. William Blake, engraving of the 'Ghost of a Flea', from Varley's *Zodiacal Physiognomy,* 1828.

139. William Blake, *The Soul hovering over the Body reluctantly parting with Life,* 1805. Tate Gallery, London.

139

THE DIVINE PRINCIPLES

Blake, Varley, and the spirits of the past

WHEN WILLIAM BLAKE drew fairies circling the head of blind Milton in his illustrations to *Il Penseroso*, he was drawing creatures he had experienced, not merely figments of his imagination. As he put it himself:

> A Spirit and a Vision are not, as the modern philosophy supposes, a cloudy vapour or a nothing: they are organised and minutely articulated beyond all that the mortal and perishing nature can produce.[1]

All the various levels of the spiritual world, from the darker confines of hell to the rarified realms of heaven, were matters of everyday perception to Blake. Thus, in his famous description of a fairy funeral which he observed in his cottage garden at Felpham, where he lived for a while in delighted isolation from his native London, he is most matter of fact:

140. William Blake, *The Ghost of a Flea*, c. 1819. Tate Gallery, London.

> I was walking alone in my garden, there was great stillness among the branches and flowers and more than common sweetness in the air; I heard a low and pleasant sound, and I knew not whence it came. At last I saw the broad leaf of a flower move, and underneath I saw a procession of creatures of the size and colour of green and gray grasshoppers, bearing a body laid out on a rose leaf, which they buried with songs, and then disappeared. It was a fairy funeral.[2]

Similar descriptions of visions, and of the 'hidden' world of fairies, spirits and celestial beings (figure 139), abound in Blake's writings and art, yet they are frequently dismissed as 'mere imaginings', presumably because of the common modern belief that fairies and the like do not exist. Blake, however, insisted that the higher world does exist as a reality and that indeed 'Vision or Imagination is a Representation of what Eternally Exists'. . .[3] It is scarcely surprising that such a man should have developed a profound interest in occultism, for he had access to the soul world which is the proper domain of the occultist (figure 140).

140

141. John Varley, *The Castle of Chillon, Lake of Geneva, c.* 1830. Victoria and Albert Museum, London (with detail).

141

All four individuals who most profoundly influenced Blake's thought and art were occultists. The German Boehme, who dominated seventeenth century mysticism, and the Swedish spiritualist Swedenborg, who profoundly influenced occult thought in the nineteenth century long after his death, had a formative influence on Blake: Agrippa von Nettesheim, the youthful encyclopaedist of occult ideas who stood at the end of the mediaeval period, and that revolutionary esotericist Paracelsus, who was Agrippa's contemporary, were both familiar to Blake through their writings.

The influence of the first two is generally recognized. It is indeed often difficult to separate Boehme's ideas from Blake's own highly personal imagery, and though Blake wrote trenchantly against certain of Swedenborg's spiritual ideas, which he considered 'materialistic' and misinformed, nonetheless various aspects of his teachings stayed with Blake throughout his life.[4] Both Boehme and Swedenborg had the same facility as Blake in being able to enter at will into direct perception of the spiritual world normally inaccessible to man. All three claimed to speak with angels with the same facility that an ordinary man might speak with another in the street. In particular, Boehme's influence upon Blake was profound, though this has not been fully explored—largely because Boehme himself is difficult reading, and many of his ideas have been misunderstood or remain unappreciated.[5] Yet in the face of this, a penetrating study of the influence of Boehme on the remarkable Freher, the German theosophist's most able commentator—an influence which was transmitted directly to Blake through the occult illustrations in Law's edition of Boehme—confirms the importance of the German in the field of symbology:

> Actually, the procedure on Boehme's part of finding manageable and nonarbitrary symbols for the primal elements of his natural metaphysics represents a unique historical step in the presentation of philosophical thought academically recognised as such in history.[6]

Agrippa's youthful books on magic are a quarry of mediaeval occult ideas, and have always been fundamental texts for anyone interested in magic and occultism. Several of the ideas from Agrippa's text, and even one or two of the illustrations to it, influenced Blake's thought and design.[7] The indebtedness to the revolutionary ideas of Paracelsus is even more marked: in addition to certain eschatological traits, Blake took from Paracelsus the important idea of the 'Imagination', in its occult sense.

To some extent, since these four figures stand sentinel to the European occult tradition, it is understandable that Blake should have been influenced by their writings. What is surprising, however, is that Blake should have formed such a strong and productive friendship with the water-colourist and draughtsman John Varley (figure 141), who was a fine astrologer, with an amateur interest in occultism. The relationship between the two was especially important for Blake, for it brightened the last few years of his life: yet the fact is that it must have been their common interest in occult matters which drew them together, for in almost every other way they were totally different personalities.

Their lifestyles were quite different.[8] Varley was careless with money, and whilst he earned a great deal, he went through it quickly and wildly, and was constantly in debt: Blake lived on the verge of starvation, and was always in great poverty throughout the whole of his life, yet he never owed a penny to anyone. Varley was surrounded by many friends, numerous patrons, a whole school of students, and a teeming household of children: Blake had few friends, even fewer patrons, no students until very late in life, and a frugal, childless household.

Their approach to art could hardly have been more different, for even when Blake produced landscapes—the speciality of Varley—he did so in imagery redolent of his unique cosmic vision. An example of the spiritual differences may be seen from figure 141. Blake adds an elusive intensity, related to the occult tradition noted on page 74 (figure 142), by presenting his moon-light landscape with two different light sources: the trees are lighted from above right, suggesting that there is sunlight, whilst the crescent of the moon shows that the sun is in fact to the left, below the earth!

This visual duality works deeply into the subconscious of the spectator, and partly accounts for the 'intensity' within this gem of engraving. Such an occult or cosmic approach is a far cry from the mundane one of Varley, who used his delightful fluency with watercolours to depict the material veil known to what Blake called 'the mortal and perishing eye'. Varley would never have seen or drawn the fairies in Felpham, but he might well have painted a picture of Blake's quaint cottage by the seaside there.

Yet, in spite of such differences, from the time in 1819 when the two were introduced by Linnell, one of Varley's pupils, they became close and constant companions. The

142. William Blake, wood engraving for Thornton's edition of Virgil's *Pastorals,* 1820.

143. Detail from Durer's woodcut of figure 92, with 'wrongly' orientated moon.

142

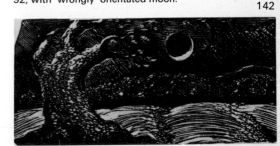

143

relationship led to great things for certain of the students around Varley—notably of course for Palmer and Calvert—and to a new warmth in Blake's relatively isolated life.

Varley's influence on water-colour painting has frequently been underestimated. While his work is uneven in quality, the finest of his drawings and watercolours rank with the greatest of any age. His influence was enormous: not only did he have among his large number of pupils such artists as Mulready, William Hunt, John Linnell and Samuel Palmer, but he helped with advice David Cox and Peter de Wint, among others, and was one of the founder members of the important Society of Painters in Water-Colours. Described as 'the very backbone of the English School of water-colour', his reputation has been marred by the vast number of inferior works which pass under his name—many painted by pupils, some potboilers done under the terrible conditions of a debtor's prison, where Varley frequently repaired. 'Things at last arrived at such a pass that he did not feel all was right unless he was arrested for debt at least once or twice a month', his biographer tells us. His debts have led some historians to describe him as an irresponsible spendthrift, but it seems more likely that he was generous to a fault, and was more frequently than not in prison because of bills he had signed on behalf of other people. This generosity and warmth he turned to good account with Blake, and his friendship had an influence in a somewhat surprising direction, for it appears to have given a new outlet for Blake's concern with the occult.

There was a rich exchange between these bizarre characters, yet to a large extent the relationship between them has been misunderstood by art historians. The curious 'seances' held by the couple, now immortalized in the series of drawings and the painting (figure 138), have been given an undue emphasis in conventional accounts, whilst the importance of the introduction of astrological ideas to Blake has been largely ignored. In many respects both the 'seances' and the astrological contributions have been misunderstood, and a re-assessment of the role played by Varley in Blake's life is needed.

In fact, there is no more revealing commentary on the difference between the art of Varley and Blake than the sketchbook which the two artists used in common. In the pages of this book we find Blake's 'portraits' of spiritual beings, which he claimed to have perceptible before him as he drew, alongside the pencil marks of Varley who was attempting to practise geomancy, the means of predicting

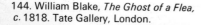
144. William Blake, *The Ghost of a Flea,* c. 1818. Tate Gallery, London.

144

the future by raising spirits through the operation of earth materials.[9] (In the nineteenth century geomancy was practised fairly widely through the random markings of pencil strokes). Blake was using the pencil to describe what he *saw* on the spiritual plane: Varley was using the same pencil in a fruitless attempt to reach into the spiritual plane through geomancy (figure 145).

The 'seances' which the two friends held together at Varley's house in Great Titchfield Street, London, are justly famous, but have not been well understood. During these sittings Blake, exercising his clairvoyant abilities, made a unique series of spirit drawings (figure 144), with Varley, unable to see the spirits being drawn by Blake, looking over the artist's shoulder in admiration. It is quite clear from the records, and from the large number of surviving drawings of spirits, that Blake was practising a variant of the curious art of *sciomancy*, involved with the raising of shades of the dead:[10]

To describe the conversations which Blake held in prose with demons, and in verse with angels, would fill volumes, and an ordinary gallery would not contain all the heads which he drew of his visionary visitants. That all this was real he himself most sincerely believed; nay, so infectuous was his enthusiasm, that some acute and sensible persons who heard him expiate shook their heads, and hinted that he was an extraordinary man, and there might be something in the matter... The most propitious time for those 'angel visits' was from nine at night till five in the morning; and so docile were his spiritual sitters, that they appeared at the wish of his friends. Sometimes, however, the shape which he desired to draw was long in appearing, and he sat with his pencil and paper ready and his eyes idly roaming in vacancy; all at once the vision came upon him, and he began to work like one possessed.[11]

There is no encounter with a 'visionary visitant' more famous than the one with which Blake chose to call 'the ghost of a Flea'. Blake painted this visitant at full length (figure 140) in a tempera panel, and drew its portrait in the sketchbook shared with Varley (figure 144): this drawing was later engraved by Linnell and reproduced in a book on astrology by Varley (figure 138).[12] The story of the curious visit is recorded by Cunningham in his study of Varley, set out in the words of a 'friend' who was in fact none other than Varley himself. The draughtsman has just been showing Cunningham a book of spirit drawings done by Blake, including portraits of a spirit who had

145. Plate of geomantic characters from F. Barrett, *The Magus*, 1801.

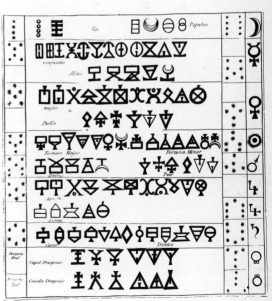

114

called himself Pindar, the courtesan Lais, and Herod:

> He closed the book, and taking out a small panel from a private drawer, said, 'This is the last which I shall show you; but it is the greatest curiosity of all. Only look at the splendour of the colouring, and the original character of the thing!' 'I see', said I, 'a naked figure with a strong body and a short neck—with burning eyes which long for moisture, and a face worthy of a murderer, holding a bloody cup in his clawed hands, out of which it seems eager to drink. . . But what in the world is it?' 'It is a ghost, Sir—the ghost of a flea—a spiritualisation of the thing!' 'He saw this in a vision then?' I said. 'I'll tell you all about it, Sir. I called on him one evening, and found Blake more than usually excited. He told me he had seen a wonderful thing—the ghost of a flea!' 'And did you make a drawing of him?' I inquired. 'No, indeed,' said he. 'I wish I had, but I shall, if he appears again!' He looked earnestly into a corner of the room, and then said, 'Here he is—reach me my things—I shall keep my eye on him. There he comes! His eager tongue whisking out of his mouth, a cup in his hand to hold blood, and covered with a scaly skin of gold and green;' (—and he described him as he drew him).[13]

The 'panel' which Cunningham held in his hands is now in the Tate Gallery, London (figure 140), whilst the original drawings have recently been found in the communal sketchbook which had been lost for almost a century.[14]

The drawing of the flea was used to illustrate a paragraph in Varley's book on zodiacal physiognomy, in effect to illustrate a Geminian facial type (figure 138). It was probably Varley's idea to link Blake's flea with the sign Gemini: the fact is that Blake's drawing bears little resemblance to a flea at all, though it does have some proximity to a true Geminian face.[15]

It is hardly surprising that modern art historians have attempted to trace this curious drawing to material sources with which Blake could conceivably have been familiar, and in spite of Blake's insistence that he drew it from a vision he had of the spiritual world. For example, Peter Tomory[16] claims that the ghost, 'despite Varley's account of its creation' is an écorché (flayed) study of an etomological specimen, whilst Martin Butlin[17] has suggested that Blake had in mind the illustration of a flea which was printed in Robert Hooke's *Micrographia* of 1665 (figure 146).

The fact is that the engraving of an enlarged flea in the

146. Micrographic enlargement (engraving) of the head of a flea, from Robert Hooke, *Micrographia*, 1665.

147. Plate by Freher from William Law's edition of Boehme, *The Works of Jacob Behmen, the Teutonic Theosopher, 1764–1781.*

Schem xxxiv

146

148. William Blake, *The Body of Abel found
by Adam and Eve, c.*1826. Tate Gallery,
London.

148

Micrographia shows not the slightest resemblance to Blake's drawing, and it is hard to see why a comparison has been made. The other suggestion, that the drawing is an écorché study, raises the inevitable question 'of what?'—certainly it is not of an écorché flea, assuming indeed that fleas may be flayed.

Such attempts as these to pull Blake's art from the Imaginative sphere into the material, by far-fetched visual analogies, reflects the uneasy state of modern art criticism in relation to the occult. With particular reference to Blake, the general impression appears to be that, since it is not possible to see spirits (and this, in spite of the vast literature to the contrary), then Blake must have been fooling with Varley. Such opinion misses the whole point about Blake as an artist.

Since there may be little doubt that Blake had the ability to practise sciomancy, and to conduct seances, the intelligent question to be asked of his art is, 'What kind of spirits was he drawing, and from which part of the spiritual world did they come?'. In the accounts given by Blake and his friends of the 'visitants', any informed occultist recognizes the appearance of 'elementals', low grade beings which inhabit the lower levels of the astral plane, and which are capable of partial materialisation.[18] The sketchbook drawings (figure 144) suggest that the visitants were of the low order which the American spiritualist Davis called *diakka*,[19] 'morally deficient and affectionally unclean' spirits or shells of human beings who had passed into the spirit world after death.

This series of spirit drawings is not unique as sciomantic works, but they are unique as spirit drawings from the hand of a master. There is admittedly a slightness about their execution which has been remarked upon by Blake scholars, but it is unfair to dismiss these drawings because of any technical weakness—they are unique as experiments, were drawn by oil lamp or candlelight, and there is no artistic criterion by which they may fairly be judged. There may be no doubt that Blake had an atavistic clairvoyant vision which removed him at once from the understanding of those limited by an ordinary view of the world. Gilchrist, the mystic's early biographer, was remarkably perceptive in his assessment of Blake's vision, and in discussing whether or not Blake was mad, he writes:

For Blake was, in spirit, a denizen of other and earlier ages of the world than the present mechanical one to which chance had rudely transplanted him. It is within

149. Detail of *The Ghost of a Flea* (figure 140).

149

150. Blake's horoscope, from the magazine *Urania*, 1825.

151. Zodiacal woman, from Ebenezer Sibly, *A New and Complete Illustration of the Occult Sciences*, 1790.

152. Detail from colour plate 147—the triangular motif on Freher's plate.

153. William Blake, *Newton*, 1795. Tate Gallery, London.

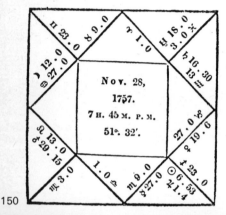

150

151

the last century or so, that 'the heavens have gone further off', as Hazlitt put it. The supernatural world has during that period removed itself further from civilised cultivated humanity than it was ever before—in all time, heathen, or Christian. . . It is *only* within the last century and a half, the faculty of seeing visions could have been one to bring man's sanity into question.[20]

Varley and Blake were undoubtedly working closely together when such drawings were being made, when geomancy and sciomancy were being practised, and when Blake was raising ghosts with his magic pencil to bewilder future art historians. The hand of Varley in this matter is beyond doubt, and whilst his artistic influence upon Blake was minimal, there are signs that his astrological influence might have been considerable. At all events, shortly after his meeting with Varley, Blake began to introduce into his compositions elements which, whilst certainly present in the Boehmian symbolic systems, were deeply entrenched in the astrology practised by Varley.[21]

That Varley should have practised the art at all is remarkable, in view of the times in which he lived: the great tradition of English astrology which had been established in the seventeenth century, largely as a result of the work of such men as Lilly and Gadbury, had by the beginning of the nineteenth century all but petered out.[22] The only useful books on the subject were those by Sibly,[23] and it is probably from one of these that Varley learned the art (figure 151). At all events, as Alfred Story says, astrology gripped deeply at Varley's soul:

> Every morning, as soon as he rose, and before he did anything else, he used to work out transits and positions for the day, or what astrologers designate 'secondary directions and transits'. Thus he would work up his own horoscope for the day.[24]

Such terms indicate that Varley was able to exercise the difficult art of astrological prediction—an art which at that time appears to have been almost lost. There are several stories of his abilities as a forecaster of coming events: one of the most fascinating is that concerning Varley's interest in the newly discovered planet Uranus, which had been discovered by Herschel in 1781. This planet was then something of an enigma for astrologers, since they had not yet been able to determine its influence in charts: the general impression was that it represented a disruptive and violent power in a horoscope. Varley was himself of the opinion that the planet was likely to unleash a disruptive force in his own life, when a certain configuration was triggered off in his own horoscope. He calculated that this should reach its maximum influence at about twelve o'clock in the afternoon of a certain day. In view of the threatened peril, Varley decided to stay in his studio, but when a few moments before the predicted time nothing had happened, he decided that it must be his property which was threatened by the malignant planet:

152

> Just then there was a cry of fire outside, He ran out to see what was the matter, and found that it was his own house that was in flames. 'He was so delighted', said his son Albert, describing the occurrence—'he was so delighted at having discovered what the astrological effect of Uranus was, that he sat down while his house was burning, knowing though he did that he was not insured for a penny, to write an account of his discovery. He had timed the catastrophe to within a few minutes. . .[25]

Varley never hid this interest in astrology, and whenever he met someone for the first time, he invariably made a note of their birth data, in order to cast their horoscope. Blake was obviously interested in Varley's methods, especially in his concern for the meaning in the ancient symbols, and he presumably gave permission for the publication of his own horoscope by Varley (figure 150).[26]

In some of his notes and marginalia, Varley shows an interest in the symbolism of the astrological sigils,[27] an interest which Blake followed in regard to the symbols and sigils used by both Boehme and Freher. It is often overlooked that when Blake said of Freher's engravings in Law's edition of Boehme (with what was for Blake superlative praise), 'Michael Angelo could not have done better', he was referring to engravings which consist essentially of astrological, alchemical and arcane hermetic symbols and sigils.[28] His attraction for such symbols was consistent with his interest in the prolix literary, alchemical and astrological symbolism of Boehme and Paracelsus which virtually all Blake scholars recognize as the very stuff of Blake's imaginative form.

It is probable, for example, that the triangular design traced by Newton in figure 153—and indeed the insistent triangular form of the dividers in his hand—are related to the occult symbols used in Freher's plate (figure 152). This 'occult' triangle is at once the astrological *trine* aspect—a symbol of the harmonic numerical relationship between cosmic points—and also the esoteric symbol for elemental Fire, which is associated with the human intellectual faculty. The very rigidity of the symbol contrasts with the

153

154. Analysis of triangular structures in Blake's *The Body of Abel found by Adam and Eve.* (See colour plate 148)

154

curvilinear forms of the composition of *Newton*, and suggests that through his work on harmonics the mathematician is bringing Fire to the Earth, in an image of a latter-day intellectual Prometheus.

It is certain that with such an 'astrological and occult' interest in symbolism being brought to the fore, there is no accident in the fact that after his meeting with Varley, Blake began to sign some of his drawings with the sidereal time, using astrological symbolism. Similarly, he began also to incorporate certain astrological and alchemical symbols into his imagery in such a way as he had up till now introduced them into his writings. At least one important picture, which he painted the year before his death, is based entirely on a hidden compositional device which owes its inner meaning to the astrological symbolism. This is the remarkable panel, *The Body of Abel found by Adam and Eve* at figure 148.

One must from the outset dismiss the immediate thought that this painting is illustrative of the Bible. The subject matter happens to be intimately bound up with Boehme's occult cosmo-conception, specifically with his highly personal view of the role played by Cain in human evolution, and the role of Evil in human life.[29] In view of this, an appreciation of the hidden alchemical and astrological symbolism within the structure of the painting requires some examination of Boehme's view of the first murder.

In his *Three Principles*[30] Boehme applies his personal exegesis to the story of Cain, whom he sees as a symbol of everyman, separated from God, as a prototype of the individual who chooses to dwell in the material world— who delights in incarnation: he is the first man who 'built his earthly Kingdom' in this world rather than in the world spiritual. Both Boehme and Blake find significance in the fact that the Lord condemns Cain to be a fugitive and vagabond on earth, for this is seen by them as the state common to all human beings who are removed from the presence of God.

The contrast established between Cain and Abel is reminiscent of Boehme's seminal experience of the spiritual world, when he perceived that the entire material world of experience (the 'Outworld') is a result of the struggle between the *Fierceness* and the *Meakness*.

And here the two strong Kingdoms of the Eternity are to be seen, which have been in strife with one another, and are always so; and the Strife continues to Eternity, for it is also from Eternity, viz. (between) the Fierceness and the Meakness. If the Fierceness was not, there could be no Mobility; but it overcomes in the World only according to the Kingdom of Hell, and in Heaven it makes the ascending Joy, and the Meakness.[31]

Within the Boehmian cosmo-conception, man's perpetual agony on the physical plane ('My punishment is more than I can bear' cries Cain in *Genesis*) arises from the fact that he reconciles within him both the angelic nature and the demonic, both of which find an uneasy union on the physical plane:

> There is nothing in Nature, wherein there is not Good and Evil; every Thing moves in this double Impulse, Working, or Operation, be it what it will. But the holy Angels, and the fierce wrathful Devils, are here excepted; for these are severed apart: Each of these lives, qualifies, and rules in his own peculiar quality.
>
> The Holy angels live and qualify in the *Light*, and in the *good* Quality wherein the Holy Ghost reigns. But the Devils live and reign in the *fierce* wrathful Quality, in the Quality of Fierceness and Warmth, Destruction or Perdition.[32]

When through his 'crime' Cain descended further into the earthly condition and alienated himself from the angelic condition, he took into himself the painful qualities proper to the fierce demons. It is this experience of the *Fierceness*, and its separative effect, which Blake emphasises in the painting: Cain's agony in the burning, and his 'mobility', are contrasted with the spiritual stillness of Adam and Eve. Blake demonstrates these two polar opposites through a secret symbolism rooted in astrological and occult lore.

One of the hidden symbols is intended to reflect the conflict between the Meakness and the Fierceness. The curiously arranged group of Adam and Eve, lamenting the dead Abel to the right of the composition, is carefully designed to fit into a triangular shape (figure 154): the archetypal male and female are united within the triangle in order to indicate their stability and harmony as a pair still bathed in the light of the spiritual world. Unlike Cain, they did not elect to 'go out from the presence of the Lord'.

On the left-hand side of the picture, the dramatic posture of the desperate Cain is contained within another triangle (figure 154): in this case, however, the triangle rests on its apex, with the agonizing face near the centre. Not only is an inverted triangle unstable—and therefore evocative of what Boehme terms 'mobility'—but it is the reverse of the structure containing Adam and Eve. This

155. Detail from Freher's plate (figure 147) showing the so-called 'Seal of Solomon', the two interlocking triangles which represent the union of the four elements around the invisible quintessence.

155

156. Plate from Law's edition of Boehme
(1764–1781). The plate has several paste-
down flaps, which reveal 'inner' occult
associations.

156

inverted triangle represents the instability and agony attendant upon separation from God, whilst the right half represents the stability of God's spiritual presence.

The two triangles, stable and unstable, are used as symbolic devices in one of the hermetic diagrams in the edition of Boehme with which Blake was familiar (figure 155), intended to form a graphic synopsis of Boehme's cosmo-conception.[33]

The quality or *Outpouring*[34] of Light is symbolized as a triangle resting on its base, expressing the idea that 'Meakness is a still rest'. The Outpouring of Fierceness is symbolized as a triangle balancing on its apex, expressing the idea that the 'Fierceness in every power maketh all things moveable, running and generative'. In Blake's painting, these overtones of associations between the triangular forms and the Light and Fierceness are too clear to be accidental: the 'Fierceness Triangle' which encloses Cain is part of the running figure, surrounded by the flames from which dark clouds are issuing—a fine graphic resolution of the image given by Boehme of 'Dark Fire', which Blake linked with Hell. The contrast between the *solar light* and the *dark fire* of hell is one of the underlying themes of Boehme's writings, but the graphic interpretation of these themes which Blake used—in the image of the sun and the smoke-flames around Cain— were probably derived from the *Third Table* reproduced in Law's edition of Boehme. The flap at the feet of the man standing to the left of figure 156 pulls down to reveal the monstrous demons in hell (figure 157): from this hell arise flames and smoke which curl up the figure of the microcosmic man as far as the circle depicting the celestial world on his back. This is a striking occult image of the teaching that man is rooted in hell, yet at the same time linked with the stars.

The basic triangular form is also one of the basic constituents of astrology, for it is used to denote the *aspect* called a trine, which is an angular relationship between two or more planets separated by 120 degrees. The underlying philosophy of this aspect is that two planets so separated must be working through the same elemental nature, expressing their natures harmoniously through the pact within the elements.[35] This astrological symbol could account for Blake's adoption of the triangle motive in his tempera panel: on the other hand, it could also account for Boehme's own personal imagery. Without supporting evidence it is difficult to be sure whether Blake was working through the occult tradition or through the

157. Detail of figure 156, with the lower circular flap folded back to show man rooted in demonic activity, with the flames of hell investing his form.

157

astrological.[36] The intimate relationship between Boehmian imagery and the astrological makes it impossible to separate the strands of the imagery within this picture, even within the framework of the refinements of the secret symbolism which Blake further elaborates.

The two Outpourings of Light and Fierceness interact in Boehme's view to produce a third Outpouring, called *Conflict*. In terms of another level of imagery, the Light World and the Dark Fire World together produce the *Outworld*, the sublunar world where the four elements interact. This meeting of Meakness and Fierceness produces what Boehme calls the *Kreuzrad*, a revolving motion.[37] In the beautiful plate engraved by Dionysius Freher (figure 147) the interaction of the two triangles is portrayed less dramatically than in the Blake painting, yet within each—one of which is inverted, one stable on its base—there is a circle which symbolizes the rotation of this *Kreuzrad*. These two circles suggest more than rotation, for they are graphically linked with the modern solar sigil (☉) now universally used in astrology to denote the Sun, but which was accorded a graphic etymology by Agrippa linked with the idea of rotation![38]

Blake adopts this idea of using a circular form within his two triangles, though with a subtle difference which carries his symbolism beyond anything possible for Freher.

Blake places his first circle within the *Meakness* triangle (figure 158) by arranging Eve in a curious posture, cradling the head of Abel, her own head hung down in sorrow. The curious position echoes the solar sigil, for the arms and shoulders form the outer circle, whilst the head marks the central dot (☉). In his own inimitable manner Blake has suggested that Adam and Eve remain within a state of spiritual grace of Meakness (the triangle), because their own solar principle of consciousness is united within the triangular shape.

On the side of Cain, in the *Fierceness* triangle (figure 159), the situation is different. The face of Cain remains within the inverted triangle, but it is not surrounded by a circle of spiritual consciousness: this circle stands to one side of the triangle, in the form of the separate physical sun. The visual message is at once quite clear: because Cain has sunk deeply into the Outworld of matter, where he burns in the fierceness, he is alienated from his conscious self, from his link with the solar divine. Blake is portraying Cain fleeing from his own inner being.

Within the Boehmian philosophy, the image of Cain in

158. Analysis of left-hand triangle of Blake's painting (figure 148), with Eve forming the solar glyph.

159. Analysis of right-hand triangle of Blake's painting (figure 148), with the image of Cain separated from his solar consciousness (the outer circle) symbolized the separate disk of the sun.

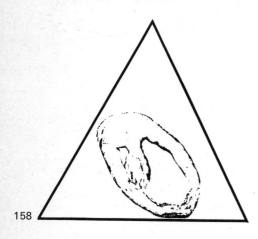

158

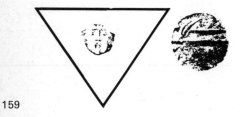

159

agony opens up thoughts not of despair, but of hope for the future, for the time when Cain will be redeemed of his Earthly burning in the 'wrath-fire' of the four elements. Man's present state is merely an aspect of time—an important concept within Blake's view—whilst he is caught in the limitations of his senses.[39] Freher's plate illustrates the fall into duality, and then into time; its consequent alienation from the spiritual world is figured in this illustration in a more diagrammatic way than in Blake's image of Cain, yet much the same philosophy underlies the images. The upper central circle, labelled *Adonais*, contains the two interlinked triangles of the Seal of Solomon, in which the two separate 'trines' are conjoined as All and Nothing in union. These two triangles are then separated into the two small circles below, and it is this separation which creates the duality of the Outworld: each of the circles pour their energies (symbolized in the outpouring vortices as the astrological aspects) into the zodiacal model below. The explanation on the banner around the Outworld explains the cause of this time-ridden condition: 'Out-breathed exhalation from spirit △ and spirit ▽ which is called time in this world'. There is no tragedy or agony here—only the message that this is the Law.

The first murder, and the consuming Dark Fire, which are the subject of this painting, reveal a message which is almost diametrically opposed to the one usually associated with the imagery of Cain. For both Boehme and Blake, Cain is the one who descended into matter, the one in whom creative forces lie—'Cain was made of flesh and blood. . . began to turn to terrestrial arts; not only to agricultural pursuits, but also to working the metals'.[40] In Blake's Genesis, the mark of Cain is the kiss of the Forgiveness of Sins, and in the genealogy of Mary which Blake constructs, the Mother of Jesus is descended from *Caina*, who was Cain's sister-wife.[41] The burning of Cain in this Dark Fire, and the genealogy of Jesus, reflect the heresy which maintains that the Messiah must consist of the worst stock if he is to plumb the depths of sin.[42] For Blake, then, the murderous Cain is the image of regeneration, an important idea which he may well have derived from Boehme himself:

> The killing of Abel's external body by Cain symbolises that the external man must be mortified in the wrath of God. The wrath must kill and consume the external image that has grown in the wrath, but from its death springs forth the eternal life.[43]

160. Detail of figure 148—the tormenting flames arising from Cain (compare with figure 157).

160

COLOURED FIRE

The occultism of Mondrian and Kandinsky

THE DUTCH PAINTER Piet Mondrian was notoriously exacting about the design of his studio, insisting that every element should express his own distinctive painterly ideas. From his early workshop in rue du Depart in Paris, through those in Holland, to his last studio in East 59th Street, New York, the interior design resembled the severe rectilinear compositions which predominate in the paintings which made him famous. His recorded intention was to create a working space which 'breathed his ideas' in the spirit of the times.[1] Towards this end, with the exception of a richly ornate stove, all ordinary furnishings were excluded: he insisted that the antiques with which other artists tend to clutter up their working spaces, thereby making them into 'museums of old art', actually prevented the artist from keeping close contact with present time.

In view of this, it is remarkable that Mondrian should permit one large photograph to be placed on the wall of his geometrically arranged room, alongside the rectangles of pure hues. This was the larger-than-life portrait of the most influential occultist of the nineteenth century, H. P. Blavatsky. This mysterious lady, a Russian of aristocratic birth, had travelled the world in search of occult and esoteric truths, and had in 1875 formed the Theosophical Society, which became the most important nineteenth century body to dedicate its energies to the study of occult knowledge, and of which Mondrian was a most enthusiastic member.

Even a brief examination of Mondrian's work (figure 162) might lead one to suspect that the artist did not wish to translate the anthropomorphic visions of theosophy into his work. Detailed analysis supports this suspicion, and not surprisingly the analyses lead not to the secrets of the Mahatmas, but to traditional compositional theory, albeit rooted in Pythagorean and Platonic notions. In fact, it is not so much in the paintings themselves that the

161. Wassily Kandinsky, *Yellow Centre*, 1926. Boymans van Beunigen Museum, Rotterdam.

162. Piet Mondrian, *Painting I*, 1920. Museum of Modern Art, New York.

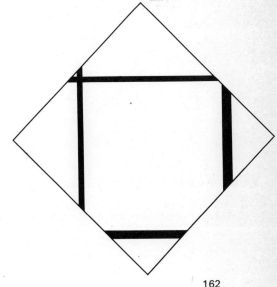

162

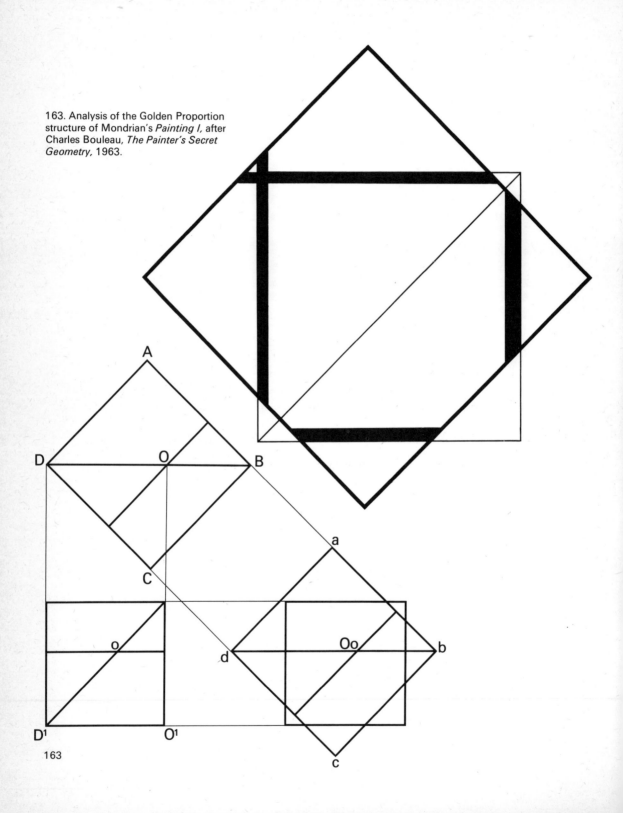

163. Analysis of the Golden Proportion structure of Mondrian's *Painting I,* after Charles Bouleau, *The Painter's Secret Geometry,* 1963.

163

relationship between his ideas and Blavatsky's theosophy are to be found, so much as in his own expressed theory of art.[2]   A geometrical analysis of certain of his paintings show them to be related directly to the Golden Section beloved of occultists.[3] Several of his more elementary compositions are dependent for their vitality upon relatively simple transposition of incompleted squares related to the divine proportion, whilst the more complicated pictures, such as the *Boogie-Woogie* series, are based upon a complex of harmonics depending entirely upon golden ratios. One analysis provided by Bouleau for his *Painting 1* sets out the logical graphic sequences by which Mondrian attempts to deal with the theme of establishing a repose which 'becomes plastically visible through the harmony of relations', as Mondrian puts it.[4]

Mondrian begins his geometric construction with a large canvas (ABCD, in figure 163), which he first cuts with a diagonal (DB), which he then bisects at a golden ratio (O). He then constructs separately from the canvas a second square with the larger part of the ratio (DO) as measure for its sides (D'O'). The diagonal of this smaller square is bisected at the golden ratio point (o). This smaller square is now laid on the original canvas in such a way as to allow the two golden ratio points (Oo) to coincide, with the diagonal of the canvas (db) meeting the parallel of the smaller square, drawn through o. This superimposition gives the basic structure for the painting itself. The thickness of the four lines within the composition, derived in their placing from the orientation, is based on a ratio of $3:4:5$, the thickest of these being derived from the intersection of the small-square diagonal with the canvas side (ab).[5]

164. Wassily Kandinsky, decorative motif used as heading for *Uber das Geistige in der Kunst,* 1912.

164

Mondrian is striving away from the representational, not merely towards a delightful decoration, a cerebral play with numbers, but towards the 'ideal'. He is consciously ascribing to the Pythagorean view of numbers when he uses such geometry to attain to the general and universal. He is opposed to the self-indulgence of his contemporary Expressionists, 'who express their own reality and not abstract reality'. Mondrian is vehemently opposed to self-indulgent art, and insists that through geometric art one may seek out higher plastic forms, in the platonic sense. He rightly understands that one must be wary of seeing in the crossing of two lines the symbolism associated with them for over two thousand years—for in so doing, one pulls the spiritual forms down to the material plane. He is in effect making a plea for the dehumanisation of art in order

165. Wassily Kandinsky, decorative motif used as heading for *Uber das Geistige in der Kunst,* 1912.

166. Wassily Kandinsky, *Lines with Rays,* 1927, Guggenheim Museum, New York.

165

166

that art may be purified of self-indulgence and materiality.

Mondrian's approach is geometric and strictly rect-ilinear, and as an art form it contrasts strongly with the highly-charged book illustrations at figures 164 and 165, which were drawn by Kandinsky, and used by him to decorate the pages of his own curious essays on art. Oddly enough, the contrast between these two different artists had a common starting point for both their theories and their practical approach. Both artists were deeply involved in occultism, specifically in the theosophy which was given its preliminary formal expression in the writings of Blavatsky.[6]

In fact, the photograph of this formidable lady in Mondrian's studio looked out onto the strange beginnings of modern non-representational art. Several of the artists of that period owed their spiritual development and in many cases, indeed, their important artistic and aesthetic discoveries, to the tenets of occultism introduced to the West by Madame Blavatsky. Mondrian's early experim-ental work with symbolism and then with abstraction owes its form largely to the writings of Blavatsky and early theosophists, whilst the geometric formalism of his late neo-plastic style was greatly influenced by the ideas of the Dutch theosophist Schoenmaekers, who developed a form of mystical mathematics which fascinated Mondrian.[7] Wassily Kandinsky, one of the other great fathers of modern art, was profoundly influenced by both Blavatsky and that most remarkable and learned occultist of the twentieth century, Rudolf Steiner, who until 1913 had been closely connected with the development of the Theosophical Society.[8] Kandinsky quotes Blavatsky, and leans heavily upon Steiner, in his own book, *Concerning the Spiritual in Art*,[9] which is a somewhat confused call for a new future form of abstraction, and a proclamation that the art of the future must be spiritual. Both these ideas arose from occult teachings with which the artist was familiar.

To some extent, at least, Kandinsky's view that the art of the future should be abstract—or non-objective, as he preferred to call it—appears to have proved correct. At all events, he was certainly right in seeing the first decade of this century as one that marked a complete hiatus in art development, for the painting and sculpture of our own time is totally different from that of preceding centuries. The major changes which have been introduced into art have in fact been inseminated by certain occult ideas current at the end of the last century. The historian

Robsjohn-Gibbings[10] has argued trenchantly and entertainingly for the massive influence in modern art of what he called 'magic' and the occult, and whilst he does show some misunderstanding of both art and the occult, he was the first art historian to point directly to named occultists as the source of the non-objective art:

> Non-objective art ... was, according to modern art authorities, a German innovation and began in Munich with Kandinsky. Actually, non-objective art began ... in the early 1900's. It is a by-product of astral manifestation as revealed in Theosophy, spiritualism and occultism.[11]

Until quite recently there has been a marked reluctance among art historians to admit the dependence of non-objective art on occult sources. This is no doubt due partly to the unpleasantly 'unacademic' sound of the word occult, and also partly due to the ignorance of most art historians as to the real nature and extent of occult teaching, which has always influenced the development of art.[12] The result is that the ordinary art-historical method has provided several 'explanations' as to why non-objective painting should have arisen when it did, but since these explanations rest on the patent fallacy that the new must somehow arise mechanically out of the old, they are unsatisfactory. Art, after all, is not the product merely of mechanical forces, but of spiritual forces influencing and inspiring the artist himself.

The term 'abstract' had been used for many years in reference to art: perhaps first by the German painter Runge at the very beginning of the century.[13] However, the word generally turns out to mean something quite different from modern contexts, when such early uses are scrutinized: it was certainly used by artists who had absolutely no intention of painting 'abstract' pictures in the modern sense of the word.[14] If the word were to be used with anything like a modern connotation for work produced before 1900, then J. M. W. Turner might reasonably be nominated the first abstract painter. By the late 1820's he was already producing canvases of emotively textured pigment which were just as far removed from the familiar world as it was possible to get (figure 167). And yet, Turner was dependent upon external Nature for his paintings, his art being rooted in love of the external world. For all the vast influence which Turner had on French painting, it required very many stages, and numerous painterly 'discoveries' before it was possible for Monet's pantheistic pictures of haystacks to be termed

167. J. M. W. Turner, *Seascape,* 1828. Tate Gallery, London (with detail).

167

'abstract'. A superficial analysis might even suggest that there is a strict line of descent from Turner, through Monet's haystacks, to Kandinsky's neo-abstraction, since the Russian himself refers to just one of the haystack series which greatly influenced him at an impressionist exhibition in Moscow.[15] However, such a connection is a tenuous one. Between Turner and Kandinsky is an unbridged gap: the two men were interested in portraying very different worlds. Turner was in love with this world, and would lash himself to masts in order to study storms, the more to grasp at Nature; whilst Kandinsky painted in his studio, depending for his ideas upon occultist theory and carefully prescribed meditative practices. Turner and his dependants looked outwards into the calm and storms of the world: Kandinsky looked inwards, into the calms and storms of the inner man. The truth of this is expressed by his friend Franz Marc, who, summarizing the reasons for the move to non-objective art, said

> . . . we were no longer restricted to the objects (of the physical world) since our knowledge had penetrated to the life which they conceal.[16]

The important sources which enabled such artists as Kandinsky and Marc to penetrate to a hidden life lay in the various occult traditions which were being made available in book form, and in various lectures, at the end of the last century.

Of the numerous artists drawn to occultism at the beginning of the century, Kandinsky offers the most satisfactory means of demonstrating the effects of such attraction. Although, unlike Mondrian, he was never officially a theosophist, his preserved list of occult books, his known reading, his continuous references to a variety of occult ideas, and his attendance at Steiner's lectures, all provide a rich documentation of the occult forces at work during his development as an artist.[17]

When Kandinsky entitled one of his paintings *First Abstract Watercolour* (which he dated 1913), he was perhaps knowingly being inaccurate. In fact, the first abstract painting was produced in watercolours some fifteen years or so earlier by a group of virtually unknown English artists—one of whom had some fame as a topographical artist—and there is no doubt whatsoever that Kandinsky had actually seen reproductions of many of their works. The first of these early non-objective paintings (figure 170) had not been made for aesthetic purposes at all. They were the by-product of experiments in painting the *astral plane*, a spiritual plane invisible to ordinary perception, but

168. Wassily Kandinsky, *Battle,* 1910. Tate Gallery, London.

168

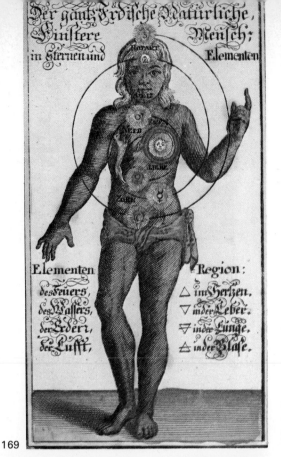

169

169. Plate from Georg Gichtel, *Eine Kurze Eroffnung und Anweisung der dreyen Principien und Welten im Menschen*, 1799.

170. Thoughtforms seen in a gambling establishment, from Leadbeater and Besant, *Thought Forms*, 1905.

171. Musical thoughtform seen on the astral plane when church organ plays Mendelssohn, from Leadbeater and Besant, *Thought Forms*, 1905.

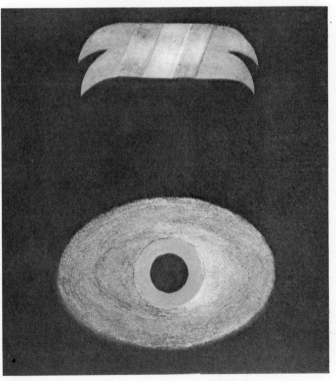

170

171

172. Thoughtforms seen at a funeral, from
Leadbeater and Besant, *Thought Forms,*
1905.

173. Wassily Kandinsky, *Woman in Moscow,*
1912. Städtische Galerie, Munich.

172

173

easily available to clairvoyant sight. A later and related group of pictures were produced to illustrate an article, and then a book, on the occult nature of human thought by the theosophists Annie Besant and Leadbeater.[18] The book was first published under the title *Thought-Forms*, in 1905, and contained over fifty plates representative of how human thought manifests itself to clairvoyant vision on the astral plane. Kandinsky owned a German translation of this text, which had been produced in 1908, and which contained the full set of non-objective pictures.

An understanding of the nature of these paintings requires some familiarity with the astral plane itself. The term *Astral* had been chosen by mediaeval alchemists to denote the sphere immediately above the ordinary physical plane, and stretched as far as that sphere in which it was believed the fixed stars were embedded: the word was roughly the equivalent of 'starry'. In his anthology of occult teachings and traditions concerning this plane, the clairvoyant Leadbeater writes:

> It has often been called the realm of illusion—not that it is itself more illusory than the physical world, but because of the extreme unreliability of the impressions brought back from it by the untrained seer. This is to be accounted for mainly by two remarkable characteristics of the astral world—first, that any of its inhabitants have a marvellous power of changing their forms with Protean rapidity, and also of casting practically unlimited glamour over those with whom they choose to sport; and secondly, that sight on that plane is a faculty very different from and much more extended than physical vision. An object is seen, as it were, from all sides at once, the inside of a solid being as plainly open to the view as the outside.[19]

In his description of the scenery and inhabitants on the Astral Plane, Leadbeater notes the existence of colours beyond the range of ordinary vision:

> one curious and very beautiful novelty brought to his notice by the development of this (higher) vision . . . the existence of other and entirely different colours beyond the limits of the ordinary visible spectrum, the ultra-red and the ultra-violet rays which science has discovered by other means being plainly perceptible to astral sight.[20]

This artistically important view that the Astral Plane might be perceived in terms of 'higher octaves' of colour was older than theosophical literature, in fact. Indeed, many of the points raised in theosophical writings at the

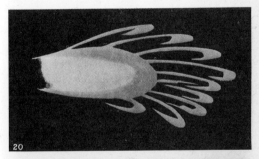

174. Thoughtforms of 'high ambition' and 'selfish ambition' from Leadbeater and Besant, *Thought Forms*, 1905.

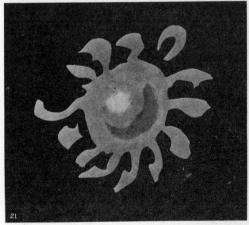

174

end of the century had been set out by a remarkable American, Edwin Babbit, in his occult classic, based on work he began in developing clairvoyance in 1870:

in a few weeks or months (my interior vision) was able to see those glories of light and colour which no tongue can describe or intellect conceive of, unless they have seen. Do you say it was imagination? But no mere imagination can come half way to the reality of these things. Imagination must construct the warp and woof of its fabrics out of realities. The finest mosaic work and the most exquisite works of art are but trash by the side of these interior splendours . . . imagination is generally more dim and shadowy than realities, but these colours were so much more brilliant and intense and soft than any colours of the outer world, and when I opened my eyes upon the sky and earth around me after seeing these, they seemed almost colourless and dim. . .[21]

The early theosophists took the problem of translating the visual appearance of this astral plane into paint very seriously, and many experiments were done in this direction. The nature of these early attempts to paint the astral plane has been preserved by both Besant and her biographer,[22] and it seems that particular work was done in connection with painting the so-called 'thought-forms', or astral images which were thrown out on to the Plane in the course of thinking. Naturally, these thought-forms were invisible to ordinary sight, but Leadbeater could see them clearly, and was able to give precise descriptions of what he saw. He and Besant would describe the appearance and colours of these forms to attendant artists, who would then make sketches and mix colours until some approximation to the original thought-form was reached. After the artists had revised the work at leisure, the work was further corrected, and 'the most successful attempt that had hitherto been made to present these elusive shapes in the dull pigments of earth' was completed.[23] The artist had needed 'coloured fire', as Besant put it, but had to make do with 'ground earths'.

The two authors of *Thought-Forms* named three artists involved in the production of these first non-objective paintings: Mr. Prince, Miss MacFarlane and John Varley. Almost nothing is known about the first two, but in any case, it is clear from later fragmentary references that the main participant in the venture was Varley.[24] In view of the fact that this 'astral painting' verged on seance work, it is a most curious coincidence that this John Varley was a grandson of his more famous namesake, the astrologer

175. Thoughtforms of 'watchful and angry jealousy' (top figure) from a double plate in Leadbeater and Besant, *Thought Forms*, 1905.

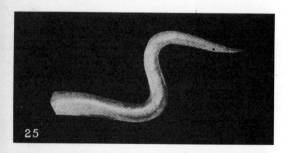

25

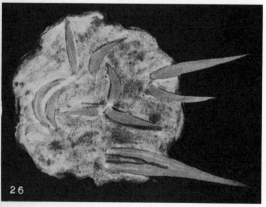

26

175

friend of William Blake (see page 111). It would seem that the Varley line had a penchant for experimenting in the drawing and painting of the astral realms.

The experimental work produced by this curious collaboration between the clairvoyants and Varley II were of considerable importance to art, if only in so far as they influenced Kandinsky into experimenting with non-objective work himself. The set of paintings produced during this period have been described as 'the first non-objective representations' which 'comply with Kandinsky's basic requirement that the artist should disregard the physical appearance of matter in favour of the psychic reality of the spiritual'.[25]

The pictures of astral 'thought-forms' range from the simple images which result from a process of 'vague pure affection' (which gives a cloud-like wash of pink), or 'watchful and angry jealousy' (which gives a brownish green, serpentine form, with a 'remarkable resemblance to the snake with raised head' (figure 175) to more complex images, such as those depicting the attitudes of loser and winner in a gambling establishment (figure 170), or the highly contrasting pair of thought forms observed by a clairvoyant at a funeral (figure 172). According to the clairvoyants, in the shape, colour and outline of the form to the right, one sees expressed nothing but profound depression, fear and selfishness. The fact that death has approached so near has evidently evoked in the mind of the mourner the thought that it may one day come to him also, and the anticipation of this is very terrible to him; but since he does not know what he fears, the clouds in which his feeling is manifested are appropriately vague. His only definite sensations are despair and the sense of personal loss, and these declare themselves in regular bands of brown-grey and leaden grey, whilst the curious downward protrusion, which actually descends into the grave and enfolds the coffin, is an expression of strong selfish desire to draw the dead man back into physical life.[26]

There is much evidence that Kandinsky's development as a painter, and indeed, his emergence as a 'non-objective' artist, was influenced by these images. Sixten Ringbom,[27] in his own appraisal of Kandinsky's dependence on occult theories, shows that the series known as the *Deluge* were deeply influenced by the abstract emanations of the so-called 'musical plates' painted by Varley for *Thought-Forms*, the images of the astral forms hovering over a church whilst specific pieces of music were being played on the organ and being observed by the clairvoyants for

176. The organ music of Wagner, seen on the astral plane, from Leadbeater and Besant, *Thought Forms,* 1905.

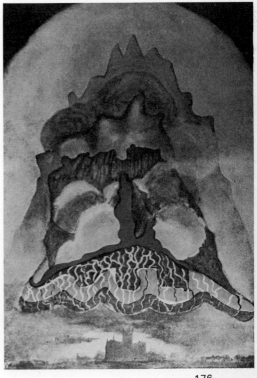

176

posterity (figure 176).[28] The pieces were by Mendelssohn, Gounod and Wagner.

It is in Kandinsky's canvas *Woman in Moscow* (figure 173) that one finds the first irrefutable evidence not only of the imagery of thought-forms, but also an intelligent use of occult imagery. This *Woman in Moscow*,[29] painted in 1912, is the earliest known major work of art to depict in abstract terms a human being standing in relationship to a higher level of the astral plane.

The canvas is exactly square, and almost central to it stands a woman wearing a white, red and orange dress. In her left hand she holds a flower, perhaps a rose, and with her right hand she is caressing a small white dog, itself curled upon a table top. At first glance it may be assumed that the woman is standing in the middle of a wide street, which is painted in an outrageous perspective of houses of a motley hue. Perhaps, however, she has her back to a window, overlooking the strange street. Behind her, and above the domesticated dog, is a figure in a red cossack jacket, and above him, running in what is called the 'flying gallop' is a dog-like creature, which appears to be barking at a sombre carriage drawn by a white horse.

Behind this cosmopolitan and consciously ill-defined assortment of figures are two large areas of paint which appear to have no relationship with the world depicted on the canvas: the handling of both these areas are 'abstract'. At the bottom right of the picture, emerging from the telluric colours below, is a rose and red blotch of paint: in the top right is a large mass of black, which appears to be either swallowing, or covering up, a large spot of red, which is itself cradled in a series of crescented hues of yellow, white and rose. These abstract areas belong to the astral plane.

The lady is standing partly in the familiar physical world, and partly in the astral plane. This does not mean, however, that the picture is merely an illustration of a lady immersed in a sea of astral entities, such as any clairvoyant might see at any time and place. In fact, the painting proves on deeper analysis to be a philosophical reflection on the relationship which humanity holds to the visible and invisible worlds: it is a sermon on the occult nature of man.

The woman who stands in this Moscovite street is by no means presented in the ordinary way. Around her is a blue, sometimes blue-grey, aura. In places this aura is clearly defined, in other places it is nebulous. This is the 'etheric aura' (figure 177), sometimes called the 'health

177. The aura of man surrounded by emotive forms, from Leadbeater, *Man Visible and Invisible*, 1908.

178. Piet Mondrian, *Devotion*, 1908. Haags Gemeentemuseum (with detail of thought form).

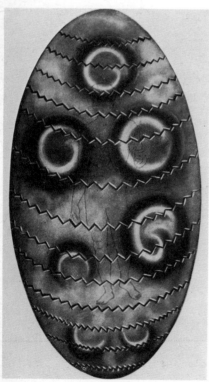

177

aura' by the early theosophists, and the 'body of etheric formative forces' by later anthroposophists.[30]

Descriptions of the etheric aura were to be found in several books which were published in the first years of our century: indeed, one of the most interesting of such texts had a fold-in frontispiece which depicted the top part of the aura in splendid colours.[31] Most frequently, however, such texts were illustrated with simple line drawings, indicating the vague enclosure of etheric forces around the body, as in figure 177. In painting the aura, however, Kandinsky need not necessarily have been influenced by such diagrams, since the spiritual exercises and meditations he is reported to have practised would certainly have enabled him to see such auras for himself. The very mobility of this aura around the woman in itself suggests first-hand experience, rather than a derived graphic source, for the aura is a constantly changing pattern of 'forces', and in no way static. Whilst Kandinsky had experimented with painting such etheric forces previously to his *Woman in Moscow*, it is likely that Mondrian made the attempt before him. Certain drawings and paintings produced by the Dutchman in 1908 clearly attempt to include images of etheric forces: his *Devotion* of figure 178 which was painted in that year actually incorporates into the etheric forces around the child an image of a thought-form.

According to occult theory, one of the important functions of the etheric body is to circulate and absorb the solar forces in our 'atmosphere': these forces are taken into the etheric at a centre approximately above the sacrum, along the spine, and then are distributed throughout the body along a series of wheeling centres, called *chakras*. A schematic representation of the movement of the *chakras*, and the two polarities of forces attached to its workings, is commonly given in oriental diagrams as two interweaving lines, running up the centre of the body through the *chakras* themselves, as in figure 179. It is probably the existence of such diagrams which account for Kandinsky's series of meander lines which he has painted on the front of the dress of the lady, as though these were part of the decorations.[32] Kandinsky was insistent upon this arrangement of two meanders, as they appear in both the glass-painting and the watercolour versions of this subject.

Kandinsky has sheathed his woman in an etheric body, and charged it with the potential power of the solar forces, and indeed with the *Kundalini*, or serpent power, associated with the oriental diagrams such as figure 179.

178

179. The Chakras of the Subtle Body.
Gulbenkian Museum of Oriental Art,
Newcastle.

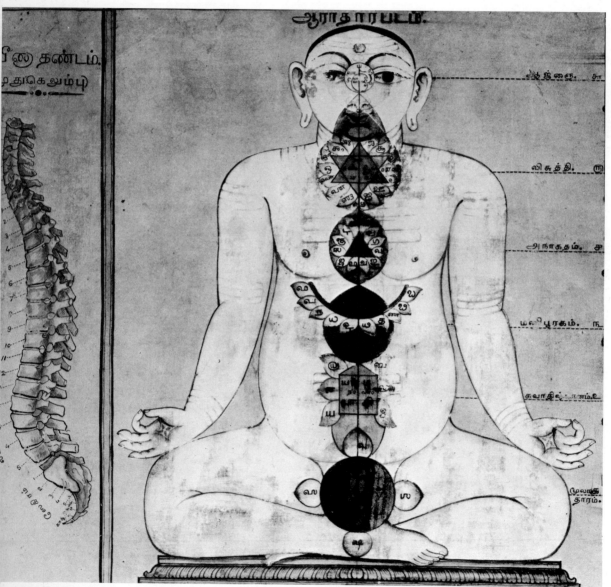

By such symbols, he removes the woman from the physical plane, and immerses her in a spiritual atmosphere: the symbols he has adopted towards this end are all derived from modern occultist thought. However, in order to reflect upon the woman's relationship to the planetary forces, Kandinsky makes use of a graphic reference to a more ancient occult tradition, in establishing a connection with a Rosicrucian image which depicts man as the centre for planetary influences (figure 180). In order to understand the relevance of this plate from Gichtel[33] in the present context, it is necessary to examine the symbolism of the various elements around this lady in Moscow: especially must we consider the flower and the dog.

The flower symbolizes the etheric forces, the 'vegetative' forces of early occultism (see page 67), whilst the dog symbolizes the astral forces (see page 67). In terms of the occultist view of evolution the vegetative world is enmeshed in the workings of the etheric forces only, and has no developed astral life of its own: these etheric forces promote growth, and maintain life on the physical plane—they do not, however, induce emotions or feelings.

The animal world, besides being enmeshed in etheric forces, is immersed also in the astral world, which promotes a rich emotional life, called the 'desire life'. In occult iconography a dog is frequently used as symbol of the 'desire' world of the astral plane.

The woman herself stands between the flower and the dog (figure 181): since she has physical growth and an emotional life, she participates in the etheric and the astral. She has, however, the higher principle of the Mental Body, which makes her specifically human.[34] As though to emphasise the mental level of her being, which is associated with creative imagination, Kandinsky has painted on the level of her head two precisely formulated thought-forms, of the carriage and the barking dog.

Within this clearly formulated hierarchy of being, one may not be surprised to find a symbol of the material plane itself—that is, matter devoid of the etheric, astral and mental qualities. This symbol is the table upon which the dog is lying so comfortably: the curiously formed legs, which are almost root-like in structure, reach into the depths of the dark, earth-bound colours at the base of the picture.[35]

The apparently haphazard arrangement of forms in the central part of the triangular composition is both interesting and purposive. It is possible to trace among

180. Diagram of the flow of energies between the chakras, from Leadbeater, *The Chakras*, 1927.

181. Detail of Kandinsky's *Woman in Moscow* (figure 173)—the decorative motif on the dress links with the chakra diagrams, the spiral structure of the flower, couchant dog, man, running dog and troika with the spiral of figure 182.

180

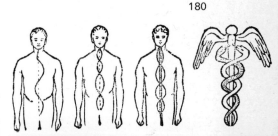

181

them a distinctive centrifugal spiral which issues from the breast of the woman and travels through the bodies of the symbols themselves, through the etheric flower, the astral dog, into the standing human form to the right of the woman. This expansive spiral movement is caught in the arch of the running dog, which may be taken as a symbol of uncontrolled astral manifestation—that is, of strong emotions undirected by the controlling mind.

The obvious spiral of this central part of the composition is perhaps influenced by the spiral in figure 182, with which Kandinsky was no doubt familiar. The illustration shows the 'ordinary' man, and maps out the occult relations which the etheric body holds to the four elements and the planets of the solar system. Not only does this picture immerse the man within the astral world, in the same way as Kandinsky immerses his woman, but it clearly links the symbols of this astral world with a spiral formation. Of immediate interest is the fact that both plate and painting give a dog to the right of the figure, and furthermore a dog in precisely the same flying gallop, and in the same size ratio to the figure. The fact is, however, that Gichtel gives no indication in his extensive commentary as to what this dog symbolizes, and it is only when the structure of the spiral itself is disregarded that it is possible to grasp its true meaning.

If the spiral in Gichtel's plate (figure 182) is visualised as moving centrifugally from the Sun (that is, from the heart, with the snake curled around it), then the spiral order is Sun, Venus, Mars, Mercury, Jupiter, Moon, Saturn, in terms of the symbols drawn on the various centres. This order, or course, bears no relationship to the order of the planets seen from an ordinary vantage point.[36] However, there is a meaningful order in this arrangement. The leaping dog is level with the Sun, which is a kind of fulcrum for the group. Below this pair we find Venus, Mercury and the Moon: these are the 'planets' which have their orbits between the Earth and the Sun. Above the dog-Sun, we find Mars, Jupiter and Saturn, the three planets which in Gichtel's day were the only known ones in orbit beyond the Sun. From these elementary astrononomical facts, it is clear that the running dog is a symbol of the Earth itself!

The peculiar strength of this symbolism lies in the fact that the dog itself is running clockwise, whilst the movement of the snake, curled around the heart, is widdershins. The dog must therefore symbolize the natural direction of the earth-bound desires—the urge

182. Detail from Gichtel's plate at figure 169.

182

which all occultists regard as being involutionary, and opposed to the spiritual urge of the Sun. The running dog represents the downward, earth-bound desires in man and earth.

There may be no doubt that the rich levels of symbolism in Gichtel's plate, which represents Natural Man standing within the planetary spheres, which are also working within his whole being, must have been in Kandinsky's mind whilst he painted *Woman in Moscow*. Many of the compositional changes which Kandinsky has introduced into his picture indicate that the lower natural animal—symbolized as a dog—which is at once a part of the inner world, the outer world, and the astral plane, may be tamed. Kandinsky's picture suggests that the involutionary direction in man may be completely changed and rendered evolutionary, through the control of man's higher faculties.

The hints on the symbolic level are confirmed by the thought-forms in the astral atmosphere.[37] In Kandinsky's painting, the spiral discharges itself into the space between the two great masses of thought-forms which represent the polarities of the human state—malice and affection. The graphic message conveyed in this discharge of the spiral must surely be that the process of evolution which has led man through the equivalent of plant-life, through the astral-life of animals, and which has now invested him with the mental faculty, must be seen as giving rise to inner conflicts which between them seek to pull man downwards and upwards at the same time. The struggle between these two forces (which, as theosophical literature insists, are 'entities' on the astral plane), symbolized as the struggle between black and red, must be the chief preoccupation of ordinary men at this point of evolution.

Kandinsky's picture deals not only with the past and present, but also with the future. It indicates that man is not merely composed of a physical body, rooted in the fourfold elemental kingdom, but that he stands astride the vegetable and animal kingdoms, towards which he holds responsibility, through his higher mentality. In terms of the future, the imagery is so arranged as to point to man's cosmic function as a meeting point between the two conflicting polarities of the spiritual world which must be reconciled by man.

Woman in Moscow is by no means an abstract picture, but its iconography permits one to trace convincingly the influence of occult ideas concerning the nature of man and the spiritual world, sufficiently to see the direction in

183. The 'directed affection' thoughtform below the troika of Kandinsky's *Woman in Moscow*. (See figure 173)

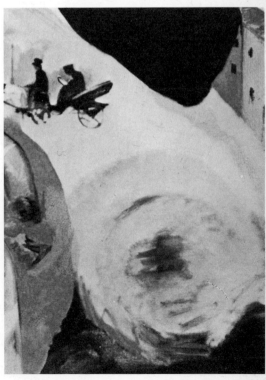

183

184. Wassily Kandinsky, woodcut *Composition II*, 1911, with detail to show rider on horseback.

185. Wassily Kandinsky, lithograph, *Composition I*, 1925.

184

which Kandinsky was leaning. He is aspiring to paint the spiritual world of the astral plane, the sight of which is 'a faculty very different from and much more extended than physical vision'.[38] In developing his own spiritual vision, he is led to the painting of structures and forms totally foreign to ordinary perception. At a later stage in his career he will create forms which totally exclude the physical plane: for the moment, with *Woman in Moscow*, he is attempting to bind together a vision of the spiritual by means of the physical plane.

After this seminal period in Kandinsky's development, he becomes more involved with the invisible astral plane, with the forces which have 'a marvellous power of changing their forms with Protean rapidity'. By the year after *Woman in Moscow*, his canvas *Landscape with Church* is only tenuously connected with a 'real' landscape, and with forms which loosely resemble a church—they are also, incidentally, stylistically linked with the music plates of which figure 171 is an example.

In the later series of paintings, the familiar world of experience is completely dissolved in the astral forces which maintain that world: unless this is fully appreciated, his work will not only remain an enigma, but its intentions will not be understood at all. Without an understanding of the relationship between Kandinsky's painting and the occult view of the world, it is possible to dismiss the whole of his later paintings with his own contemptuous phrase as 'mere aesthetic decoration'.

There is a world of difference—a spiritual world of difference, so to speak—between the subject matter of the woodcut at figure 184, which Kandinsky printed in 1911, and the lithograph at figure 185, which he printed some fourteen years later. In the first, various elements from the material world are recognizable—the riders to the foreground, for example—but in the second there is nothing which might reasonably be linked with the material plane, though of course a strong fantasy may trace in its form a semblance to a human being. The difference between the two does not lie in the subject matter, so much as in the intentions of the artist: in the one case he is striving to give an aesthetic expression to elements derived from the physical; in the other case, he is striving to give expression to something he feels or perceives in the spiritual spheres, a thing which may or may not have a more or less tenuous connection with the material plane. It is this important difference which severs much of the art of our own century from that of the past.

185

l'inquiétait; il en fut sévèrement repris par le prophète Elisée.

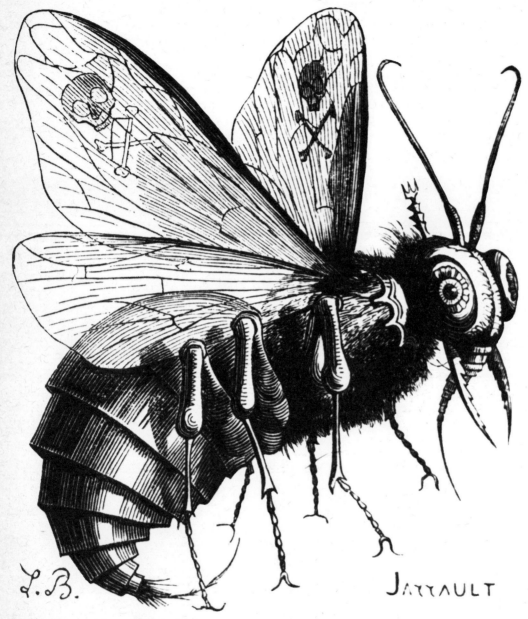

On lui attribuait le pouvoir de délivrer les hommes des mouches qui ruinent les moissons.

AS ABOVE, SO BELOW

Aspects of alienation in modern art

WHEN THE GERMAN painter Max Ernst was about fifteen years old, his pink cockatoo died. On the same day his sister was born. He later recorded that for some time he remained irrationally convinced that these two events were connected, the birth being a result of the death, or vice versa. The impression left upon him by this slip in the normal grasp of causality stayed with him for a long time, and perhaps even helped form his later view of art. At all events, his biographer John Russell saw more than casual significance in the experience, and wrote:

> An auxiliary result of this double incident was that Max Ernst became more than ever interested in magic, and in the occult, and in every sort of arcane (and most often forgotten) wisdom.[1]

Actually, Ernst was never an occultist himself, nor did he ever align himself with any esoteric body, as did Kandinsky and Mondrian, yet throughout his life he maintained an interest in occult imagery, with the result that various devices within his paintings and collages are intended to convey hidden meaning.

One example is a page layout which Ernst designed in 1941 for a bulletin on modern art and poetry.[2] In the double page spread Ernst provides a list of his favourite poets and painters: the names include such poets as Baudelaire, Blake, Goethe, Shakespeare and Whitman, as well as such painters as Breughel, Bosch, van Gogh, Seurat and da Vinci. The surrealist element in the design—the Ernst touch, so to speak—was that he placed at the head of these groups of names two bizarre images of the evil spirits derived from a popular work on demonology.

These two demons (figures 186 and 187) were taken from de Plancy's rambling and not wholly reliable text on occult matters, the *Dictionnaire Infernal*,[3] which was lavishly illustrated with the kind of grotesque wood engravings that provided Ernst with a wide choice of illustrations from which to select his demons. This point is

186. Beelzebub. Wood engraving from Collin de Plancy, *Dictionnaire Infernal,* 1862.

187. Andras. Wood engraving from Collin de Plancy, *Dictionnaire Infernal,* 1862.

187

188

worth making because, whilst Ernst's choice might have been 'accidental' (whatever that means, in the context of art), it may be inferred that he wanted to convey a meaning through his choice of these particular images. Certainly, since these demons are treated at length by de Plancy in the text from which Ernst abstracted the images, we may be sure that he was familiar with the reputations and traditions attached to them.

Ernst placed *Beelzebub* (figure 186) in his physical manifestation as 'Lord of the Flies' above the poets, and the demon *Andras* (figure 187) above the painters. According to the witch-hunter Wier, *Beelzebub* was the Prince of Demons, but the poet Milton, following the biblical tradition, placed the demon second to Satan in power.[4] The curious tradition concerning the origin of the demon's strange name is relevant to Ernst's choice, for the sixth century historian Psellus[5] informs us that it was derived by converting *Beelzebul,* which signifies 'God in Heaven' into *Beelzebub*, which means 'God of the Dunghill', suggesting the idea of a creature fallen from Godhead, with the physical appearance of a huge fly, and a propensity to delight in ordure.

The denigration involved in this play with one letter of a word made *Beelzebub* an appropriate demon for Ernst to associate with the name of poets, whose business is words, for he was of the same iconoclast outlook as the Dada painters who attacked the cultural traditions upon which our civilization is founded. The implications in the imagery of figure 186 is that poetry was merely a 'play with words', under the rule of a fallen god.

The choice of *Andras* (figure 187) to head the painters was equally felicitous, since this was the demon conjured by those magicians who sought to kill their enemies. It is possible that in this choice of image, Ernst was reflecting on the prevalent opinion in his circles that the art of the past was an enemy of any art of the future, and should be destroyed. A particularly poignant strength is added to this association of *Andras* with the painters, for in his short autobiographical notes, Ernst had announced his own death at the beginning of the First World War:

Max Ernst died on 1 August 1914. He returned to life on 11 November 1918, a young man who wanted to become a magician and find the myths of his time.[6]

Perhaps, in this page design, Ernst is adopting the role of magician, and conjuring *Andras* to destroy the artistic enemies listed below the image.

The implications of this simple mis-en-page are an

expression of the cultural chaos which had perturbed artists during the early decades of our century, especially those gathered under the banner of the Dadaists, Surrealists (figures 188 and 189) and the Futurists, who felt and expressed an overwhelming urge to destroy the foundations of the society and the art upon which they had been nurtured. There could be few clearer indications of the break which had taken place between the art of the past, and that of our century. In previous times artists had certainly rebelled against what they saw as feeble or weak, but they never rebelled against society as a whole. The impressionists of the nineteenth century suffered a deep feeling of alienation, and no small degree of bitterness, but the overall feeling was that they did really belong to society, and that, 'However keenly they felt the state of separation imposed upon them by society, they remained convinced that it was nothing more than a misunderstanding'.[7] The post-War years held no such conviction for many artists: the majority of them felt that the new world they wished to build could not be constructed save over the ashes of the old—and in the conflagration which would destroy the evil, would perish also all that which had hitherto been regarded as useful, good and beautiful.

After 1910 it was as though the spiritual world which held so much promise for Kandinsky had withdrawn. Artists accustomed by tradition and inclination to speak on its behalf fell into an anguish of despair. There was no shortage of material excuses for this despair—the World War, the political and social conditions, and all the eternal trappings of injustice, suffering and inequality which are woven into the very fabric of human existence. However, the anguish arose not merely from such external conditions, as from the fact that the ancient role of the artist had come to an end: the artist had no longer a niche in society, or even a real purpose in the exercise of his art.

This despair speaks in the art and lives of very many artists during this period, and in all the major art 'movements', from Futurism, which hid its spiritual agony in the vociferous welcome of materiality (a vociferous welcome too loud and insistent to ring true), to Surrealism, which quickly degenerated into what one of its finest exponents described as a visual game, based on 'the paranoia of the double image' (figure 189).[8]

The apt phrase is Dali's, and it is perhaps no accident that his most famous picture, *The Metamorphosis of Narcissus* (figure 188), is concerned not only with double images, but with the nature of the creative act.

188. Salvador Dali, *The Metamorphosis of Narcissus,* 1934. Tate Gallery, London. Reproduced by permission of the Edward James Foundation. (With detail of Narcissus)

189. Detail of the Dali at figure 188— Narcissus transformed into a hand.

189

190. Detail of the Dali at figure 188—dog eating offal, and the chessboard motif.

191. Fay Pomerance, *The Sixth Palace of Hell,* 1945. Private Collection.

190

The body of narcissistic man (gazing at his own reflection in the waters, but perhaps seeing nothing) is transformed into a 'double' of a hand (figure 189), which is surely a symbol of human creativity. His head is transformed into an egg, which hatches out a narcissus, at once a symbol of that self-love which propels ordinary human thinking, and a symbol of the yearning for light.

Oddly enough, the physical body of Narcissus is actually *in* the water (that is, deeply within the subconscious) rather than on the bank, as in the original story. This would suggest that Dali is pointing to the conflict—in the contrast of images—between the 'lower' forces from which art springs, and the higher intellect. Such an interpretation is supported by the image to the right (figure 190), for at the base is a dog, nosing through offal—a fine symbol of the lower urges, reminiscent of the image of Mars (figure 106): above this dog is a large chessboard, a rather obvious symbol of the human intellect. In this double imagery we have a fine presentation of the crisis of identity in art, for the picture raises the question of the relationship between the two polarities—between the dark waters and the light-striving intellect—which are found in every human being, but which are intensified in the artist.

Most of the modern schools of art proved that the ancient art was dead: their very intellectualism, their defence of soi-disant 'isms', their iconoclast urge, and their sad dependence upon journalistic techniques, first in the belligerent manifestos, and later in the proliferation of gallery catalogues, apologias, monographs and art books. These alone indicate the extent to which the medium that was supposed to be pictorial and visual was being usurped by the medium of words.

Within such a context, it was a stroke of genius for Ernst to place two demons over the arts. The situation has changed little in over thirty years. The artist has been pulled away from his meaningful, if lonely, struggle, and he is now helplessly caught up in a maelstrom of influences, disputes and superficial verbiage, with a maiming demand for 'originality' which, if it means anything at all, generally means that the artist has no longer anything worth saying. The demons no longer permit the time, the spiritual space, for the development of that need for meditation and reflection which Kandinsky saw as the basic requisite of a new art.

One of the few paintings of recent times which has succeeded in setting out the tragedy of this receding spirituality is Ernst's masterpiece, *Of this man shall know*

When the time comes for an evil man to die
LILITH appears to him and induces him to sin with her
and during his sin she kills him

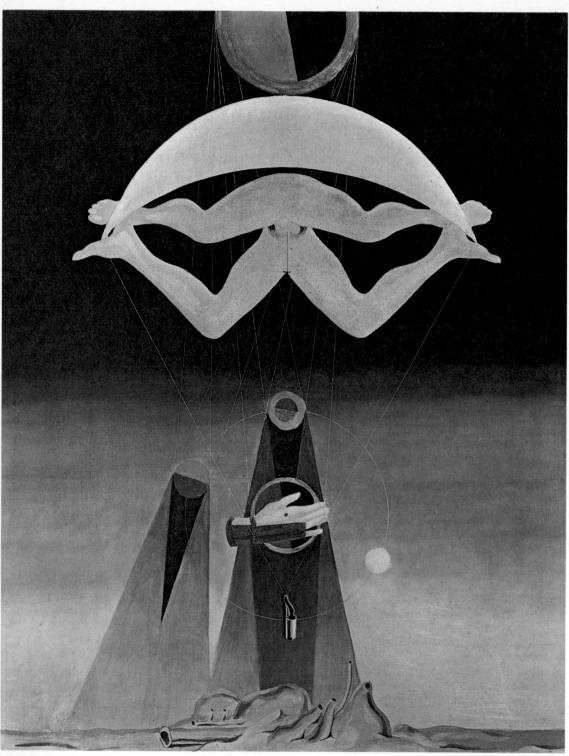

nothing[9] (figure 192), which he painted in 1925. Perhaps it is the symmetry of the composition which imparts to the canvas a classical quality which encourages Russell to describe it as one of the two Ernst paintings which 'could hang with European paintings of many periods, without regard to subject-matter, and not lose their dignity'.[10] However, this symmetrical 'classical' surface hides a storm of graphic and philosophical implications, and in this respect Ernst is merely working within accepted techniques of metaphysical painting, as set out by his friend Chirico:

> The appearance of a metaphysical work of art is serene; it gives the impression, however, that something new must happen amidst this same serenity, and that other signs apart from those already apparent are about to enter the rectangle of the canvas. . . For this reason the flat surface of a perfectly calm ocean disturbs us, not so much because of the idea of the measurable distance between us and the sea bed, but more because of all the elements of the unknown hidden in that depth.[11]

The 'element of the unknown hidden in the depth' of Ernst's canvas is intended as a consistent statement of man's relationship to the universe, for the subject of this canvas is the age-old occult theme of 'man the microcosm' (figure 193)—though here it is a mutilated man, portrayed as a fragmented being, in a fragmented macrocosmic desert. The old occult adage, 'As Above, so Below',[12] is given an ironic twist.

It is significant of the direction which art has taken that, whilst Kandinsky could portray man's relationship to the spiritual world in the recognizable image of a woman standing in a street, only fifteen years later Ernst could portray man's relationship to the spiritual world through an entirely dehumanised image, in which the complete man himself is missing, his recognizable fragments mutilated. This study of dehumanization is conducted within a denuded landscape, shrouded in the acceptable forms of symmetry, classical allusion, perfect harmony of spatial rhythms, and the muted harmonic hues, designed precisely to hide a secret symbolism as potent and horrific in its reflection on the inner life of man, as any of the worst nightmares of Bosch or Goya. In this respect, *Of this man shall know nothing* is the last of the truly great occult paintings.

The strange imagery of this painting is to some extent explained by an inscription on the reverse:

The sickle moon, which is yellow, and like a parachute,

192. Max Ernst, *Of this man shall know nothing*, 1923. Tate Gallery, London.

193. Cosmic man, from William Law's edition of Boehme, *The Works of Jacob Behmen the Teutonic Theosopher*, 1764–1781.

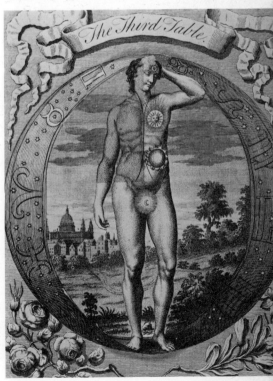

193

194. Sandro Botticelli, *Venus? c.* 1505.
Staatliche Museen, Berlin.

194

prevents the little whistle from falling to the ground. As it is being treated with respect, the whistle believes that it is rising up to the Sun. In order that it might revolve better, the Sun is split in two. The model is stretched out in a dreamy posture. The right leg is bent forward in a precise and pleasing movement. The hand shields the Earth. This gesture endows the Earth with the significance of the sexual organs. The Moon runs at great speed through its phases and eclipses. The picture is unusual in its symmetry. The two sexes maintain each other in a state of balance.[13]

It is typical of Ernst that the words of this dedicatory poem explain nothing about the painting on an ordinary level—indeed, they render interpretation more difficult. For example, on first scrutiny, it is not immediately apparent that these are the legs of a model, nor is there any sign of the 'two sexes' to which Ernst refers. Again, the 'phases of the moon' to which Ernst refers are not painted correctly, nor is the 'model' stretched out in a dreamy position—it is a four-legged monstrosity pinned down in a kind of nightmare. There may be no doubt that Ernst has his tongue in his cheek when writing in such a way about the obvious surface symbolism.

However, the inscription does prove to be meaningful if the picture is examined from the correct standpoint, as a meditation on the nature of man's relationship to the cosmos.

The painting is geocentric—that is, the pivot of the fast-spinning moon is the earth. The position of the hand which covers this central earth is itself significant, for as Ernst says, 'This gesture endows the Earth with the significance of the sexual organs': the hand covers the earth in a gesture reminiscent of the coy act of the Venus nudes of Western art, seeking to protect their pubic area from the prying gaze of men, a gesture which may be traced back to early Christian art forms, in which the fallen Eve hides her private parts from the sight of God or Adam, because she knows that she is naked. Through these associations with nakedness, sexuality and the 'Fall', the gesture is linked with insecurity. In Ernst's painting the hand is partly disguised to look like a glove: indeed, it is only on Ernst's written authority that we know that it is intended to be a hand at all. This is the inversion of the ordinary function of clothing, which is to disguise the body, and to hide the sexual parts: in this image, the hand itself is disguising the body, and yet it is partly disguised itself. With a simple image of a partly covered glove, set within a circle, which is itself placed over the earth, Ernst has constructed a brilliant new symbol for the idea of the guilt which is inherent in all human beings.

André Breton, to whom this painting was dedicated, later wrote a few notes about the function of surrealistic painting, describing it as 'the systematic putting out of place',[14] which was a more concrete verbal equivalent of the famous poetic description of Lautréamont:

Beautiful as the chance meeting upon a dissecting table of a sewing machine with an umbrella.[15]

Breton chose a hand as an example of how the super-reality may be reached:

to put a hand out of place by isolating it from an arm, that hand becomes more wonderful as a hand: and in speaking of the 'lonely displacement' we are not thinking only of the possibility of moving in space.[16]

The fall of man, which is echoed in the image of this severed hand, is symbol of the severance of the human being from God—a 'lonely displacement' from the spiritual worlds which gave the pre-Fall couple sustenance. The pain and agony depicted by Blake in his image of burning Cain is dehumanised by Ernst to the level of a severed, gloved hand—an exceptionally suitable symbol for man's creativity, since it is with the hand that the artist puts his ideals into physical expression. The 'lonely displacement' of which Breton speaks is not merely one of space, but one of spirit—the hand is severed from creativity, from contact with the spiritual, which is to say that it is as meaningless as the block of marble from which the Venus who makes the same protective gesture is herself carved.

To the right of this hand-covered earth is a moon, bathed in its own shadows. To the left of the earth, the same moon casts no shadow! This left-hand moon casts no shadow precisely because it is a glowing light-source itself. Ernst, in suggesting that either the moon has been transformed from dead materiality into a molten sun, or that the sun itself has contracted to the size of the moon, is painting the solar system in chaos, and has (incidentally) reversed the traditional occult association of the left with the moon, the right with the sun (see figure 91). Instead of confusing the light source and the angle of reflection in the traditional manner, Ernst creates two different reflections—to the right is a moon bathed in its own shadows, to the left, a non-moon, shadowless, and a source of light. This is indeed celestial chaos.

The poignancy of the symbolism is deepened when

195. Detail of dislocated hand, and phases of the moon, from the Max Ernst at figure 192.

195

196. Wood engraving of the Eclipses and Phases of the Moon, from Babbitt, *The Principles of Light and Color,* 1878.

Fig. 160. Eclipses and Phases of the Moon.

196

one realises that the isolated 'hand' is placed over the earth in order to suggest that the earth itself is the centre of the sexual functions—within such imagery, the human sexual functions are also in chaos. Such sexual nuances permeate the entire composition, and largely explain the dominance of the lunar symbolism, for in the occult system, the moon regulates the human sexual function, which explains why so many hermetic images depict the crescent moon over the private parts (figure 193).

A further occult connotation is added to the arrangement of the semi-lunar orbit, for the entire image is derived from a plate in Babbitt's occult treatment of Light and Colour,[17] which influenced Kandinsky: the wood engraving (figure 196) was set in Babbitt's text to illustrate the phases of the moon. Ernst must have delighted in adding such a visual reference, not in itself occult, yet from an occult source, for this is a reversal of the normal procedure, as evinced in his mis-en-page, where he inserted occult images into a source not in itself occult.

Ernst has developed the imagery of the engraving to a point where he has been able to suggest that the two shadows and penumbras from the moon are almost like ghosts walking the sterile earth below, the central 'ghost' arising from what appears to be a pile of offal. In fact, the visual impact of this central penumbric figure is extremely powerful: its presence is felt throughout the entire picture, as a kind of 'ghost in the machine'. The tiny 'lunar' head at the top of the shadow triangle contrasts with the gigantic hand which lies across its body, whilst the tin whistle appears to hang over the place where one might reasonably expect the sexual parts to be located. That Ernst should choose a triangle to convey a sense of a 'human' form in a painting otherwise so dehumanised, in a setting which Chirico would have called 'a landscape of the Tertiary period', is in itself probably a reference to one of Chirico's own ideas regarding metaphyiscal geometry:

> ... the triangle has served from antiquity, as indeed it still does today in the theosophists' doctrine, as a mystical and magical symbol, and it certainly often awakens a sense of uneasiness and even of fear in the onlooker, even if he is ignorant of this tradition. In like manner the square has always obsessed my mind. I always saw squares rising like mysterious stars behind every one of my pictorial representations.[18]

In this painting Ernst has constructed a brilliant occult imagery which reflects upon the ancient relationship between microcosm and macrocosm, and yet which eschews the traditional approach to such symbolism, depending as it does upon a new system of visual co-ordination. On an intellectual plane—which is to say, on the plane at which it is capable of valid intellectual analysis—it shows dehumanised man as a fragmentary shadow, broken upon a cosmic wheel which is itself in upheaval.

The chaos of the 'cosmos' is reflected in the chaos of the unnatural relationship of the four human legs. The symbolism of this strange group of legs is complex, but essentially it may be discussed in terms of the traditional imagery, and then in terms of the newly constructed 'metaphysical' imagery specific to Ernst. It is part of Ernst's success as a 'magician' that he has learned to build the new upon the foundation of the old.

First of all, then, the symbolism is involved with the idea of placing the crescent moon *over* the legs. In the traditional religious and occult imagery, the female stands on the moon, to show that the regenerated human spirit has dominion over the lower and bestial lunar forces. There is a woodcut by Durer which shows the Mother and Child cradled in such a crescent moon, and its symbolism is intended to proclaim this subjugation of the lower forces to the Mother of Christ (figure 198): this is the feminine counterpart of the masculine images which show Michael subduing the lunar dragon. In this curious image by Ernst, however, the natural or supra-natural imagery is reversed: the sexual act is implied in this arrangement of legs, even though it is a sexuality of a dubious kind, with the moon in total domination over the action below. The legs are not cradled in the moon, as is the mother of God in figure 198, so much as dropping out of the up-turned crescent. The modest protective gesture of the severed hand, which is shielding the pudenda of Earth, is insufficient to drive away the demons, and the influence of the moon proves insuperable.

A second level of lunar symbolism is perhaps even more striking, and is involved with a play upon the symmetry of the picture itself. The curious arrangement of the 'four' legs, suspended from the parachute crescent, may appear to give the impression of some kind of perverted sexuality, but it is in fact merely a reflection of a pair of human legs, in a parody of the imagery attached to the story of Narsissus! If half the picture is cancelled out, with a straight edge running exactly down the centre of the picture (figure 197), then it will be seen that the pair of legs has been painted, almost in Renaissance manner, in

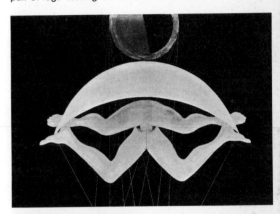

197. Detail from Ernst's painting at figure 192, with half the image cancelled, to show single pair of legs 'resting' on the crescent moon.

197

aposition which, as Ernst says in his dedication, is a 'dreamy pose', but which at the same time also suggests the feminine receptive position for the sexual act.

From this 'cancelling out' of half the picture, one sees that the female half is to be visualised as lying down on the crescent of the Moon, a posture which brings the secret imagery more in line with the occult tradition, since it introduces the idea of the moon being under the woman. However, if one attempts to study this human posture, it is necessary to turn the picture upside down, which is, of course, tantamount to turning the solar system in the painting upside down.

In fact, one must not only turn the picture upside down, but also cancel out half the painting. In doing this, one imitates the creative act of the sun, which cancels out half of any body (with shadow) by shining upon it. Ernst involves the spectator in a manipulative act which implies that the spectator is himself a kind of solar deity, though one dwelling in a cosmos in chaos.

The precise orientation of the light-dark sun at the top of the picture points to a further aspect of the 'cosmos in chaos' theme, for the diameter which separates the solar light from the solar dark is on an axial direction at a pronounced angle to the vertical symmetry of the picture. This axis points directly to the 'moon' which is to the left of the hand: since this moon casts no shadows, it may be taken as a 'sun' itself, wrongly placed in the cosmic order, and thus integrated within the 'disorder' of the lunar symbolism.[19] The topmost moon, circling the hand-earth, is dark where it should be illumined: so indeed is the moon to the right also dark where it should be lighted. This play with 'wrong orientation' is carried through even into the dehumanised human element above the lunar orbits, into the four-fold legs which are pinned to the large crescent moon.

In his dedication, Ernst had mentioned specifically the 'right leg' of the model, which he says is 'bent forward in a precise and pleasing movement'. This claim is difficult to grasp until one realises that one pair of legs is a reflection of another pair (figure 197): the pair to the left of the picture might well be the 'real' legs, the ones to the right being merely a reflection. This fact suggests that the whole painting might be intended to be a mirror image, or that the idea of 'reflection', contained in the occult maxim 'As Above, so Below', is a theme of the picture.

The visual logic of this would suggest that the dehumanised image of man, held under the domination of

198. Albrecht Durer, woodcut of *Madonna and Child with Saint John,* 1511.

199. Detail from the Ernst at figure 192, with the pile of offal in the foreground reflected in a mirror to show that it is in fact half the innards of the human body.

198

the moon, is involved with mirror imagery, on the principle that the occult tradition claims that man is himself an image or reflection of the celestial world. This man constructed by Ernst is himself a chaos, a fragmentary being without an inner centre of identity, and since this is the case, then the cosmos which he reflects must also be in chaos. Ernst carries this theme to a terrible graphic conclusion. At the very bottom of the picture he has painted a pile of offal, under the penumbra of the moon, in a curious half-vegetable growth (figure 199). This offal is itself incomplete, like all the images in this remarkable painting: it requires a 'reflection' for its completion. If a mirror is placed across the bottom of this vegetation (figure 199), the completed reflection forms an image of the human innards, with the windpipe, lungs, liver and pancreas laid bare. This indeed is a sad image of the inner world of man, under the dominion of the chaotic celestial forces!

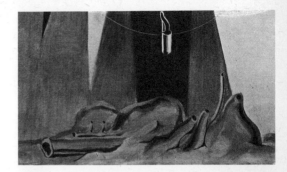

It is only within the framework of this theme of disintegration, of 'cosmos in chaos' that the full significance of the whistle which hangs from the crescent moon may be understood. This whistle is linked by lines with the tips of the crescent moon, as well as with the human feet, which might evoke associations with Piscean imagery (see page 48). However, the whistle plays no part in the circuit structures of the moons, and is divorced from the movement of the moon and earth. Ernst personifies the whistle, and tells us that it is 'being treated with respect, and for this reaon feels that it is rising to the Sun'. However, it is clear from the way in which he has painted it that it is not being drawn up towards the sun—no matter what it may 'feel'—but towards the moon. In terms of occult teaching, man's higher nature is being pulled up towards the sun, his lower nature being pulled down by the moon: man is the battleground for the struggle between the solar and lunar spirits. In addition, the only item in the Ernst picture which emits sound is the whistle: it is therefore a fitting symbol for the human being, a ludicrously pathetic image of the celestial backcloth against which it hangs.

This backcloth would in traditional occult imagery have been linked with the music of the spheres,[20] to which the life of man is a holy dance. According to platonic theory, this sound is not heard by ordinary humans in the normal state of being, because the music is omnipresent and deafeningly loud: humans are so completely immersed in this music that they are not aware of it, any more than they

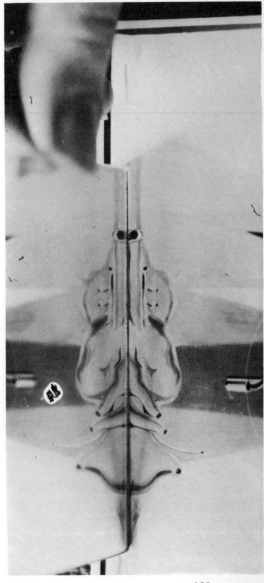

199

are under normal circumstances aware of the movement of their blood and lungs, or the sound of their own breathing.

Ernst presents us with a vision of humanity at the centre of the lunar circuits, caught in the rhythms of the solar system, and capable only of making the shrill note of a cheap whistle. The dehumanisation of man, his separation from the spiritual source, has led to a point where he no longer reflects in his inner being the majestic music of the spheres, but squeaks a shrill note of despair. Thus, *Of this man shall know nothing* (figure 192) is a magnificent metaphysical study of man's alienation from the spiritual world, a complex hieroglyphic of man's modern state of being. The formal harmony is at best merely a surface, which covers a cosmic world in chaos, with a fragmented human so disjointed as to be recognizable only through certain sexual postures and innuendos. In the heavens he is a reflected grotesque, on the earth, a pile of offal in need of a reflective surface to find a unity. The particular brilliance of the painting arises from the fact that an unprejudiced approach demands 'audience participation' in the cancelling out of areas of canvas, in the provision of mirrors, and in the inversion of personal vision.

The man portrayed here against this cosmic setting is no longer an image of the celestial worlds, no longer a noble microcosm, but a fragmentary shadow, a broken tooth of a disintegrated ratchet world. In more than one respect the onlooker is himself dragged down to this level of the fragmented imagery in attempting to correct it with rules and mirrors, reminding one of those pictures by Francis Bacon, which were varnished in order that the spectators might see reflected over the hideous imagery their own human faces. Just as the earth-man of the picture is an incomplete vegetation, awaiting a reflective surface, so is the entire painting itself dependent upon each person who examines it, brings mirrors to it, consciousness, and of necessity interacts with it, physically, emotionally and intellectually.

Ernst has successfully attacked the microcosmic image, and one feels that occult art will never be the same after this: he has made a definitive statement relating to the hermetic maxim by fragmenting images generally held to be sacred within the hermetic tradition. In many respects, this very act of violence reminds us that occult art has always depended for its strength on a repertoire of ancient symbols, sigils and ideas which are stored within the vaults of the tradition. Whilst there has certainly been a tendency

200. Alan Davie, *Entrance for the Red Temple*, 1960. Tate Gallery, London.

201. Fay Pomerance, *The Sixth Palace of Hell*, 1945. Private Collection. (See colour plate 191)

202. Woodcut from a 15th century blockbook, *Ars Moriendi Bene*.

200

in recent times for artists to mutilate such images, or to debase them by using them purely for decorative effect, as for example in the painting by Alan Davie (figure 200), which is structured around the symbolism of the doorway, and incorporates painterly versions of Christian and proto-Christian sigils, there remains a conservative occult trend in modern art which is concerned still with elements of the hidden art. Of necessity this occult art is rooted in the symbolism of the past, for modern artists tend to devote their energies to the question of aesthetics, rather than to the deepening of meaning, and the pressures of modern life are not conducive to the quiet contemplation from which true occult art grows.

A fine example of this occult art, 'rooted in the symbolism of the past', is the delicate watercolour *The Sixth Palace of Hell* (figure 201) by the modern Jewish artist Fay Pomerance.

In terms of subject matter, the painting appears to fall into the mediaeval block-book tradition of illustrations to the art of dying, which usually depict the horned lunar demons and the solar angels or saints struggling for the soul of a dying man (figure 202). In this painting the man is on his deathbed, and because his grip on the physical plane is weakening, he begins to see into the Threshold, and beholds the spiritual beings who were with him even during his lifetime. It is as though the division in the lower half of the encircled *tau* is suddenly made clear to him: good and bad are now white and black, as they have always been. The demon *Lilith* (figure 201), sitting astride *Samael*, is tempting the dying man, as she has at all times throughout his life: the difference now is that she is visible. Her fair, naked body, her rounded breast and blonde hair are intended to be sensual, for she is attempting to persuade the man to sin with her once more, in order that she might possess more fully his soul, and keep it for her world of Shells.[21]

This Lilith was in Talmudic lore the first wife of Adam, who sired upon her the demons who now persecute man.[22] She personifies the darker side of human nature, which is hidden from the light of consciousness. This dark side is represented in the right-hand vertical division of her body, which is hidden from the sight of the dying man: like the moon, Lilith is half in light, half in shadow. Her marked duality symbolizes the element of moral choice which has been confronting the human being at each moment of his life. One may be sure that when the man has finally sinned with her, then this hidden darkness will

203. Detail of *ankh* goblet, from figure 191.

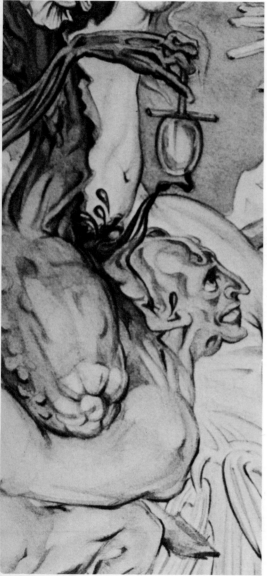

203

reveal itself to him in all its hideous aspect: when this happens, then the proliferation of organic tendril growths, plant-forms and gourd-shapes, will be recognized by the man as the demonic side of his own being.

In her hand Lilith holds a goblet (figure 203). This form is an interesting example of occult symbolizing, for it is intended to be reminiscent in shape of the ancient Egyptian *ankh* hieroglyph: ☥ Exoterically, this *ankh* is used as an amulet against barrenness, and its meaning has been explained as something like 'life which cannot die'.[23] Esoterically, however, it is associated with speech, with the Christ *logos*, and with the idea of incarnation, for occultists claim that the circular form at the top of the *ankh* is derived from the Egyptian *ru* ◯ 'the mouth or uterus of birth'.[24] This esoteric connection with the *ankh* goblet and birth is interesting because Lilith has the function of both the seduction of male souls, and the murder of new-born infants. It is probably for this reason that the artist has turned the *ankh* glass upside down so that the blood (the menstrual blood, linked with the monthly cycles, reminder of the occult teaching that the demons exist in the lunar sphere) is at once a symbol of vampirism, and of ebbing life. In this simple goblet, we see the working of occult art in a particularly illuminating form: the consciousness of the artist has allowed a free artistic manipulation of an ancient occult symbol.

The Sixth Palace of Hell is in effect an illustration to a strain of demonology found in the rabbinic tradition.[26] The angels sent by God to restrain Lilith were unable to prevent her from exercisng her role as the murderer of new-born children, but they did compel her to swear that when she saw the image of the angels on an amulet, then she would have no power over a child so protected. This legend may well be an attempt to support an ancient widespread custom of writing amulets against the child-destroyer, yet it reminds one of the recognition of the power of the image. Until comparatively recently, an image was believed to be possessed of a power far greater than its mere surface paint, for through its symbolism and secret structures it reached into the spiritual world. A painted or sculpted image was a window through which mortals might peer into higher worlds, and even bathe themselves in the healing forces which streamed from that world. The secret *tau* structure of a portal (figure 18) was working a magic in which the person who entered a church bathed himself by virtue of passing through it:[27] the secret power of the divine image was invoked through at least one picture reproduced in this book (figure 84) as a prophylactic against the plague in 1576; the curious occult sigils painted on the *trulli* in and around the lovely town of Alberobello in Southern Italy[28] (figure 204) are the degenerate remnants of this belief in the spiritual power of the image. It is this power of innocent vision which Lilith is at all times, and in all places, attempting to kill—the new birth of spirit, as much as the new birth of the child—and it is the Lilith in all of us against which art is the prophylactic.

Between the image of the men who know nothing (figure 192) and this invasion of *Lilith* from the hidden worlds, stands a huge question mark. The crisis expressed in the painting by Ernst, and the calm reliance on ancient symbolism found in the work of Pomerance, reveal something of the problem which underlies modern art. On the one hand, the artist looks into his own soul, which itself deeply reflects the loss of contact with the spiritual world, and there he finds a curious alienation from the spirit. On the other hand, he looks into the past, and sees there an art form which expresses an intimate relationship with a spiritual world which now appears to be removed from man's experience. The sensitive artist must either rebel against such a condition, or choose two creative alternatives: he must either work with the plethora of ancient symbols which, whilst undoubtedly vibrant and pregnant in meaning, no longer express the modern human condition; or he must seek out a new relationship with the spiritual world, which of necessity will lead to a new *credo* by which life may be lived, and art practised.

Whilst there are signs on all sides of the rebellion, and also of a return to the ancient symbolism, the indications of this search for a new relationship to the spiritual world are less evident. Perhaps such a search may be conducted only in private, even in secret, and perhaps the results are unlikely to find their way into the somewhat strident circles of the modern art world with its galleries which deal so openly in death, with their concern with 'aesthetics' as opposed to meaning, and their striving after the bubble reputation.[29] It is hoped, however, that such a new art is being forged somewhere, since the history of occult art leads one to suspect that the development of ordinary art, which sustains the cultural and the spiritual life of nations more deeply than our modern beliefs will admit, appears to depend upon the discoveries made by those who work secretly at the inner disciplines and meditation which are the prerequisite of the successful practise of the hidden art.

204. Symbol painted on the roof of a *trullo*, in Alberobello, Apulia.

204

205. Christ in Glory, surrounded by the
tetramorphs of the Evangelists from the 12th
century 'Royal Portal' of the West front,
Chartres Cathedral.

205

BIBLIOGRAPHIC NOTES

THE QUESTING EYE

1. R. Fludd, *Utriusque cosmi minoris et majores technica historia* . . . 1617–21.
2. This fundamental dictum is from the so-called *Emerald Tablet* attributed to Hermes Trismegistus—see J. F. Ruska, *Tabula Smaragdina*, 1926. According to the hermetic tradition there were two images of God—the Cosmos and Man: see for example, G. R. S. Mead, *Thrice-Greatest Hermes, Studies in Hellenistic Theosophy and Gnosis*, 1964, ed. Vol. 3, p. 151.
3. Leonardo da Vinci—the quotation is given in W. H. Auden and L. Kronenberger, *The Faber Book of Aphorisms*, 1962, p. 292, but no source is appended.
4. W. Kandinsky, *Uber das Geistige in der Kunst*, 1912.
5. Hildegard of Bingen, *Liber Divinorum*, P. 1, v. II. 32.
6. For a list of the more important texts by Steiner on the two Jesus children, see the notes to the Chapter on *Dual Pisces*. Steiner's highly original view of art, rooted in occult concepts, is set out in the translation of the eight lectures delivered by him in 1923, *The Arts and Their Mission*, 1964.
7. H. Krause-Zimmer, *Die Zwei Jesusknaben in der Bildenden Kunst*, 1977, p. 244.
8. See Albertus Magnus, *De Animalibus*, Lib. I, Tract. I, cap. III, in the A. Borgnet edition of Opera Omnia, 1890, Vol. 9, p. 262.
9. See the list of sources given in the bibliography on page 170 in support of my paragraph on page 89.
10. See for example, S. Ringbom, *The Sounding Cosmos. A Study in the Spiritualism of Kandinsky and the Genesis of Abstract Painting*, 1970.
11. The letterform—probably unique to sculpture in this image—is in A. Cappelli, *Dizionario di Abbreviature Latine ed Italiane*, 1899, p. 187; the Leo sigil in the forthcoming F. Gettings, *Dictionary of Occult, Hermetic and Alchemical Sigils*, Routledge and Kegan Paul, 1979.

THE LIVING BULL

1. P. D. Ouspensky, *A New Model of the Universe*, 1931.
2. Paulinus of Nola, *Poema XIX, In Natale II S. Felicis*, 1. 608–676. The relevant sections are in P. E. Testa, *Il Simbolismo dei Giudeo-Cristiani*, 1962, p. 233ff.

3. See T. Burckhardt, *Sacred Art in East and West*, 1967, p. 77ff.
4. *Revelations* 5.5. See also G. Schiller, *Iconography of Christian Art*, 1969, Vol. 1, p. 22.
5. Clement, *Recognitions* Bk. II, viii. But see also J. Daniélou, *Primitive Christian Symbols*, 'The Twelve Apostles and the Zodiac', 1964.
6. H. Kramer and J. Sprenger, *Malleus Maleficarum*: see translation by M. Summers, 1928, note on page xxxix.
7. W. Sucher, *Cosmic Christianity*, 1970, p. 4. Needless to say this speculation is not in any way related to the actual derivation of the sigil.
8. Now in the 'Renaissance Chapel' in the National Museum, Copenhagen. The carving is of inferior workmanship, and runs VERB☿M DOMINI MANET IN E TERN☿M (*sic*)—ANNON DOMINI 1582.
9. See my article 'The Dual Symbolism of Zodiacal Scorpio' in *The Mercury Star Journal*, Vol. IV, No. 3, 1978.
10. Aristotle, *De caelo*, Bk. I, ii–iv.
11. Jerome, *Lib.* 1, p. 280. Ezekiel's vision is recorded in *Ezekiel* I. 5–12. In the second century Irenaeus, *Adversus haereticos*, III, XI, 8., links the Evangelists with Ezekiel.
12. See W. C. Wright, *The Works of the Emperor Julian. Orations IV: Hymn to King Helios*, 1913, p. 404. He spoke reluctantly, this Emperor who forced his way into the Mysteries: 'It were better indeed to keep silence; but yet I will speak . . .'
13. B. L. van der Waerden, *Science Awakening II. The Birth of Astronomy*, 1974, p. 156.
14. H. P. Blavatsky, *The Secret Doctrine*, 1888 was probably the first overt attempt to synthesise science, religion and philosophy, though the text indicates that the lady had little respect for nineteenth century science.
15. See for example, A. D. White, *A History of the Warfare of Science with Theology in Christendom*, 1955, in particular I, chpt. 3.
16. For example, see W. Neuss, *Das Buch Ezechiel in Theologie und Kunst*, 1912, p. 303 ff.

17. See W. C. C. Guthrie, *Orpheus and the Greek Religion*, 1952, p. 79–86.

18. See the curious, if somewhat over-inspired, book by E. M. Smith, *The Zodia*, 1906, p. 81–83. Blake certainly had this etymology in mind when he originated his *four zoas*, his genius encompassing the brilliance of uniting in an English singular the Greek plural with more aesthetic and comfort than the mediaevals created three and four-headed figures in their painting and sculpture. There is an interesting reflection in the changes of meaning from the original *zoa*, for the word contained no evil, yet the 'beasts' which emerged from the English Version are now distinctly imagined as evil. There was more egoity in Crowley—who called himself 'The Great Beast'—than even Crowley realised.

19. Z. Ameisenowa, 'Animal-Headed Gods, Evangelists, Saints and Righteous Men', *The Journals of the Warburg Institute*, 1949: 12, 21–45, a very useful essay within the present context, but one which more than once exhibits much astrological ignorance. In this quotation, for example, Ameisenowa is off the track attempting to link the four fixed signs with the solstices and equinoxes, the former of which take place when the Sun enters Cancer and Capricorn, the latter when the Sun enters Aries and Libra. At a later point (p. 36), the same author makes Aquarius a water sign and Scorpio an air sign, and links the four *fixed* signs with the four *Cardinal* points.

20. This pulpit is probably tenth century, is now incomplete, and the priest no longer has access to the well. A large number of remarkable esoteric Christian symbols are carved on the outer well, but their interpretation would take us beyond the present context.

21. The Cardinal died in 1459, the pulpit is thirteenth century: this difference should not lead us to deny a connection between the Logos-bull and the sacrifice of Mithras, however.

22. See H. Nissen, *Orientation. Studien zur Geschichte der Religion*, 1906.

23. In the fourth century, Cyril of Jerusalem said that the supplicants turned from the West because they thereby renounced Satan, and faced the East, the place of light (*Catechetical Lectures*, xix. 9). Saint Ambrose of Milan, in *De Mysteriis*, c.ii. 7, confirms the act of turning from the West as a renunciation of the devil, to the East as a turning towards Christ.

24. W. Durandus, *Rationale Divinorum Officiorum, De Ecclesia et eius Partibus*, Section 8.

25. For example, the contemporaneous floor zodiac in the Baptistry in Florence is not dated.

26. Rounded off to degrees, the astrological data is as follows. In 1207 the extent of the Constellation Taurus was 37° to 73°: I have determined this, allowing 10° for precession and using the (mediaeval) constellation extent given in V. Robson, *Fixed Stars and Constellations*. In May 28th 1207 Jupiter was in 92° (18 Gemini), Mars in 158° (24 Leo).

Sun was 73°	29	Taurus
Moon 73°	29	Taurus
Saturn 73°	29	Taurus
Venus 68°	24	Taurus
Mercury 50°	7	Taurus

See my article 'The nave zodiac of San Miniato' in *The Mercury Star Journal*, Vol. IV, No. 2, 1978.

27. For a brief summary, see G. B. Caird, *Saint Luke*, 1975 ed., p. 16–17.

28. See L. Réau, *Iconographie de l'Art Chretien*, 1958, Vol. III, p. 828. The tradition has been 'explained' because Luke is supposed to have given more details of the life of the Virgin. In fact, the Proto-Evangelium of James gave more details of the life of the Virgin, but James was never described as a painter. An equally unsuitable explanation is more modern—that St. Luke is confused with a Florentine painter of the ninth century, who besides possessing the same name, was called *il Santo*.

DUAL PISCES

1. Julius Africanus, see Migne, *Patrologia Cursus Completus*, 1857, *Series Graeca* 10: *Africani Narratio de iis quae Christo nato in Persia Acciderunt*, p. 107.

2. *St. Luke* Ch. II. This child is often called the Nathan Jesus, sometimes the 'pontifical' child in hermetic and occult literature. A profound study has been made by R. Steiner—see for example, *The Gospel of St. Luke*, 1975 edition of translation of Basle lectures of 1909.

3. *St. Matthew*, Ch. II. The genealogy is in Ch. I. This child is often called the Solomon Jesus, sometimes the 'Royal child' in hermetic and occult literature. A profound study has been made by R. Steiner—see for example, *The Gospel of St. Matthew*, 1965 edition of translation of Berne lectures of 1910.

4. See for example the article 'Synoptic Problems' by F. J. McCool in *The New Catholic Encyclopaedia*, 1967: also the unsatisfactory article 'The Genealogy of Jesus' by J. E. Bruns.

5. See R. Graffin, *Patrologia Orientalis*, Tom. XXVII, p. 49–53: *Hippolyte de Rome sur les Benedictions D'Isaac, de Jacob et de Moise*. I was led to this important source by the article, 'Une Lettre de Simeon Bar Kokheba' by J. T. Milik in *Le Revue Biblique*, 1953, p. 291.

6. See C. Sturm, 'The Double Jesus' in *The Modern Mystic*, Feb. 1944, p. 56. The reference to Aquinas in this source is incorrect: it should be *Summa Theologica*, P. III, Q.31, Art. 3, R.3. It is clear that Sturm has not read this section, or has read it and failed to understand what Aquinas is saying: it is not an argument for two Jesus children, and in any case, Aquinas is merely quoting. He is referring to Augustine's *De Consensu Evangelisarum*. Neither of these two churchmen is intent on showing two different Jesus children so much as being concerned to show precisely the opposite, and reconcile the two different Evangelical accounts. Augustine (D.C. II. 1) follows the tradition by observing that Matthew

follows the human generation of Christ (*sic*), and later (D.C. II, 11) he says that Luke describes the priestly (*sacerdotem*) generation of Christ (*sic*). He derives the idea of *sacerdos* not from consideration of Nathan (as does Steiner—notes 2 and 3 above) but from the fact that the Luke genealogy starts at the baptism of Christ, and argues that on the evidence of John we know that the Christ was sent to bear the sins of the world, which was surely a sacerdotal office.

7. M. R. James, *The Apocryphal New Testament*, 1975 edition, p. xxiii.

8. The translation of this passage is from James (note 7 above). The translation of the *Pistis Sophia* most easily available is that by G. R. S. Mead, the 1921 edition. Actually, Ch. 61 and Ch. 62 of the *Pistis Sophia* are incomprehensible without the idea of *two* Jesus children.

9. See for example the fragment from the *Denkart* (ed. Madan, pp. 129–30) given by R. C. Zaehner, *The Teachings of the Magi*, 1975 ed., p. 96. In the form given the *Denkart* is ninth century, and *may* have been given by Adhurabadh of the fourth century, but this particular idea is obviously pre-Christian.

10. For example, the article by K. G. Kuhn, 'The Two Messiahs of Aaron and Israel', *The Scrolls and the New Testament* (ed: K. Stendahl), 1957, p. 54ff. Kuhn admits that 'The concept of the two Messiahs, a priestly and a political one, is actually not as strange as it first appears to be', yet he proceeds to miss the point of his own argument. Even so, he sees the later convergence of the three offices of prophet, priest and king, a prefiguration of the way in which the Essenes juxtaposed the three.

11. See for example *Bereshit Rabbati* by Moses ha-Darshan (ed: Albeck), 1940, p. 136. The story is told by N. Wieder in 'The Doctrine of the Two Messiahs among the Karaites', *The Journal of Jewish Studies*, 1955, p. 14–25.

12. See for example P. E. Testa, note 30. The relationship between the Christmon and the Greek *Chronos* sigil, obviously derived from *Chi* and *Ro*, as is the sigil for Christ, has not so far as I know received any academic study. An example of the sigil from a Greek manuscript may be seen in H. Omont, '*Abbréviations grecques copiées par Ange Politien*' in *Revue des études grecques*, No. 7, 1894.

13. *St. Luke*, Ch. II, 2.

14. *St. Matthew*, Ch. II, 1.

15. A. Heidenreich, *The Unknown in the Gospels*, 1972, p. 26ff.

16. O. Edwards, *A New Chronology of the Gospels*, 1972, p. 34–41.

17. The pictorial themes of the two Jesus children are discussed fully by H. Krause-Zimmer, *Die Zwei Jesusknaben in der Bildenden Kunst*, 1977.

18. See for example C. Bigarne, *Considerations sur le Culte d'Isis chez les Eduens*, 1862, who traces the black madonna to the Isis cult (p. 6ff), which he is inclined to believe was transmitted to the Romans by way of the Gauls themselves. He also notes the existence of an Isis statuette with two children, which he not unnaturally links with the astrological Gemini (p. 13). See also Fulcanelli, *Le Mystère des Cathedrales*, 1971, p. 57ff.

19. The usual 'explanation' for such iconography, that the kings represent 'Mary's ancestors', finds no canonical support. In view of the presence of Melchisedek in the lancets below, it is worth quoting *Hebrews* 7, 14–16, which is a clear reference to the two distinct lines of descent: 'For it is evident that our Lord sprang out of Juda; of which tribe Moses spake nothing concerning priesthood. And it is yet far more evident: for that after the similitude of Melchisedek there ariseth another priest, Who is made, not after the law of a carnal commandment, but after the power of an endless life.'

20. In my opinion the iconography of St. Anne has been largely misunderstood: the mother of Mary is frequently used to cover the identity of the second Mary. Art historians tend also to call all groups depicting two women with the Jesus or Jesuses (figure 66), 'St. Mary and St. Anne', without reference to the ages of the women portrayed in the groups. The mediaeval artists were more discriminating about age. However, I am not arguing in this context that this stained glass St. Anne is in fact a 'Mary figure'.

21. *Hebrews*, 7, 1–5.

22. See note 35 below concerning the 'wife of Urias'.

23. *Numbers*, 17, 1–10.

24. It may be noted that the imagery is not altogether traditional, though there may be no doubt whatsoever that Gemini and Pisces are intended, if only in view of their absence on the left door archivolt. Even the ordinary guide books do not hesitate to call them 'Gemini' and 'Pisces', though the relevance of their isolation, and the incomplete and disordered zodiac on the left door, appears to have escaped observation: see for example, E. Houvet, *Chartres Cathedral*, 1976. Needless to say, the deviation in this imagery is highly significant, though space precludes study here: the fish is a single one—perhaps unique for a symbol of Pisces—but I feel that it is intended to indicate the single union through *Christ* of the two children above.

25. Steiner attributes the origin of these mysteries to the Persian Magi, and indicates how the Virgin (*Virgo*) was linked with the two Jesus Children (Gemini) through stellar lore. R. Steiner, *The Search for the New Isis—Divine Sophia*, English translation of four lectures given in Dec., 1920.

26. See my article, 'The Sigils for Pisces and Spica' in *The Mercury Star Journal*, Vol. IV, No. 1, 1978.

27. See R. H. Allen, *Star-Names and Their Meaning*, 1899, p. 461 ff. This graphic etymology is fanciful, however: the sigil is derived from the Greek-Byzantine astrological tradition, though its present form was not realised until the thirteenth century.

28. The marble zodiac at San Miniato (see page 25 above) gives a male-female, but the Roman Mithraic zodiacs give two boys, and the Egyptian star-map at Denderah gives two males. It is interesting that the change in the imagery was paralleled by a change in sigil structure.

29. J. P. Lundy, *Monumental Christianity*, 1882, p. 130ff.

30. See P. E. Testa, *Il Simbolismo dei Giudeo-Cristiani*, 1962, p. 416.

31. It goes without saying that the constellations Virgo, Gemini and Pisces do not bear the slightest pictorial resemblance to the Virginal woman, a pair of children or to two fishes joined by a cord. The adepts who chose these astrological symbols worked through an altogether different sensibility to the one which is normally available to man.

32. The significance of such imagery escaped even the otherwise imaginative and well-informed Witkowsky (see G. T. Witkowsky, *L'Art Profane dans L'Eglise*, (*Etranger*), 1908, p. 394). Its existence leads one to question the reality of the names 'Charity' and 'Grammatica' ascribed to certain similar groups.

33. See for example R. Steiner, *The Spiritual Guidance of Man and Humanity*, 1970, English translation of lectures given in Copenhagen in 1911; and R. Steiner, *From Jesus to Christ*, 1973, English translation of ten lectures given in Karlsruhe in 1911.

34. See for example, I. Myer, *Quabbalah. The Philosophical Writings of Solomon Ben Yehuda Ibm Gebirol or Avicebron*, 1972, p. 114. These two Adams should not be confused with the two Adams of orthodox Christianity, for the Second Adam is indeed Christ. See Tertullian, *De Carne Christi*, ch. 17.

35. Jerome points out that in this genealogy appear only women censured by scriptures: *Thamar* for her sin with her father-in-law; *Rahab* for being a whore, and *Bathsheba* ('the wife of Urias') who was of course an adulteress. See Aquinas, *Summa Theologiae*, III, Q.31, Art. 3, R.5.

36. *Epistle to the Ephesians*, Ch. II, 15-16.

37. See my forthcoming *Dictionary of Occult Hermetic and Alchemical Sigils*, Routledge and Kegan Paul, 1979. Significantly, in the mss. version of Agrippa's *De Occulta Philosophia* (ed. K. A. Nowotny, 1967, p. 552), whilst mediaeval variant sigils are given for seven of the twelve zodiacal signs, Pisces is accorded only one, which is the modern form.

38. Aquinas, *Summa Theologiae*, Ia, 115, Art.4, 3.

39. See for example, M. Lund, *Ad Quadratum*, 1922 and Fulcanelli (note 18 above).

40. T. Burckhardt, *Sacred Art in East and West*, 1967, p. 48.

41. For example, Honorius d'Autun (see Burckhardt, note 40 above, p. 49).

42. The best time to study this phenomenon is in the last five days of August. I personally first observed the effect during August of 1972, but it took many visits over a period of three years to establish the rich meaning underlying this miracle of light.

43. See A. Chiarini, *La Meridiana della Basilica di S. Petronio in Bologna*, 1975.

MERCURY OF ANGELS

1. Cosimo de Medici asked Ficino to translate the *Corpus Hermeticum* of Trismegistus, before the platonic canons. See for example R. Haase, 'Kepler's Harmonies, between Pansophia and Mathesis Universalis', *Vistas in Astronomy*, Vol. 18, p. 520.

2. See the recent edition of *De Occulta Philosophia*, presented by K. A. Nowotny, 1967, which gives many of the mediaeval sources from which Agrippa worked.

3. A. Warburg, *Italienische Kunst und internationale Astrologie im Palazzo Schifanoia im Ferrara*, in *Atto del X Congresso Int. di Storia dell'Arte*, 1922, but see also P. d'Ancona, *The Schifanoia Months of Ferrara*, 1955.

4. Some of the argument may be had from R. Gleadow, *The Origin of the Zodiac*, 1968, p. 59–61; a book which is otherwise unreliable in matters of history.

5. S. Freud, *Eine Kindheisserinnerung des Leonardo da Vinci*, 1910. The merging of the two women is explained in terms of the dual image which Freud claims Leonardo had of his real and adoptive mothers.

6. This remarkable Borgognone fresco in Milan is discussed in relation to the two Jesus children imagery by H. Krause-Zimmer, *Die Zwei Jesusknaben in der Bildenden Kunst*, 1977, p. 139ff. The story runs that recent publications on the two Jesus children have resulted in so many people calling at S. Ambrogio, asking to see the 'two Jesus children' that the heretical painting has been locked away.

7. K. Clark, *Leonardo da Vinci*, 1967.

8. L. Pacioli, *Divina Proportione*, 1509. More recently, see H. E. Huntley, *The Divine Proportion*, 1970.

9. See C. Bouleau, *Charpentres, La Géométrie Secrèt des Peintres*, 1963.

10. Letter dated 13th Oct. 1506: see M. Thausing's publication of *Letters of Durer*, 1872, p. 21ff.

11. See Bouleau, note 9 above, English edition: *The Painter's Secret Geometry*, 1963, p. 101ff.

12. See for example, E. Wind, *Pagan Mysteries in the Renaissance*, 1958.

13. G. Vasari, *Le Opere di Giorgio Vasari*, ed. Gaetano Milanesi, Vol. LII, 1878. The passage reads: '. . . un'altra Venere, che le Grazie la fioriscono, dinotando la primavera, le quali da lui con grazia si veggono espresse'. This is, so far as I know, the only basis for the title of this painting, yet it is not even an accurate description of the subject.

14. The musical analysis is given by Bouleau, note 9 above, p. 86.

15. F. Gafurius, *Practica Musicae*, 1480. Gafurius had never settled in Florence, but it is evident from holograph notes that he was familiar with the writings of Ficino. It is possible that a mss. prior to 1477 was in circulation.

16. Traditionally they are Aglaia (Brilliance), Thalia (Flowering) and Euphrosyne (Joy), their father being the expansive Jupiter, their mother Eurynome.

17. M. Ficino. Quoted in E. Wind, *Pagan Mysteries in the Renaissance*, 1968. p. 122–123.

18. There is much doubt whether this picture did come from the studio of Verrocchio (G. Passavant, *Andrea del Verrocchio als Maler*, 1959), or even by a 'follower' (Davies, *Catalogue of the National Gallery. Early Italian School*, 1961). Perugino has been suggested (A. Bertini, in the McGraw-Hill *Encyclopaedia of World Art*), as well as Botticini (Berenson, *Italian Painters of the Renaissance, Florentine School*, 1963). When the panel was purchased by the National Gallery in the last century, it was believed to be by Pollaiuolo.

19. The text is apocryphal to the Protestant, canonical to the Catholic, and external to the Hebraic traditions.

20. This 'monstrous fish' of the translations was originally a crocodile of sorts: this idea survives in the latin version of the story, for in that account, when the fish attempts to swallow Tobias, Raphael commands him to catch the fish by its *arms* and drag it to the bank.

21. *Asmodeus* is said to be from the Zend *Aeshmadeva*, 'a raging fiend'.

22. It is in the *Book of Tobit* that the name first appears: the Hebrew name is perhaps from the Chaldean, meaning 'God has healed'.

23. See chapter on Dual Pisces, p. 33.

24. See the examples given in P. E. Testa, *Il Simbolismo dei Giudeo-Cristiani*, 1962.

25. Pisces shared Jupiter with Sagittarius, the sign which rules travel—Pisces being the 'day sign', Sagittarius the 'night sign' of the planet. There is a fine example of this symbolism in the Rucellai Palace, in a fresco which shows Cupid playing with the two fishes in a pictorial area dedicated to the planet Jupiter.

26. Aquinas, *Summa Theologiae*, for example, Ia, 115, 5, 3.

27. See S. Latuada, *Descrizione di Milano*, IV, 1738, p. 246.

SEX SACRED AND PROFANE

1. Origen. Quoted in G. Hodson, *The Hidden Wisdom in the Holy Bible*, 1963, Vol. 1, p. xii.

2. See for example H. Chadwick, *Early Christian Thought and the Classical Tradition*, 1966, p. 111.

3. Few good books on the subject exist. See C. Bouleau, *Charpentres, la Géométrie Secrèt des peintres*, 1963; E. C. Kielland, *Geometry in Egyptian Art*, 1955; McCody Lund, *Ad Quadratum*, 1922.

4. *Genesis*, 3.2.

5. *Genesis*, 2.17.

6. This triadic relationship has deep occult significance, difficult to discuss without prolix reference to obscure sources. Basically, the three forms of snake, trunk and arm are related to the workings of lunar forces on the earth. Tradition has it that it is the lunar forces which produce the trunk, which then flowers in 'solar' leaves and fruit: the body of man is itself merely a 'lunar' appendage to a head which has solar origins: the snake is itself the form which humanity would have adopted had the lunar forces not been removed from the Earth millennia ago. This is why the snake is such a common and excellent symbol of the lunar force.

7. For example in the lead relief of the sixth century in the Cathedral treasury at Monza (ampulla No. 13).

8. For this translation I have used the edition by P. Gall Morel, *Offenbarungen der Schwester Mechthild von Magdeburg oder das fliessende Licht des Gottheit, aus der einzigen Handschrift des Stiftes Einsiedeln*, 1869, from III, cap. IX, p. 68ff: *Von dem angenge aller dinge, die got hat geschaffen*.

9. See note 8 above. The last sentence is ambiguous: 'so emmohten wir uns von siner edelen nature sinner geschaftnisse niemer geschamen'.

10. The bull *Ad nostrum*, in Hefele-Leclercq, *Histoire des Conciles*, VI, 2, 682–4. Quoted in G. Leff, *Heresy in the Later Middle Ages*, 1967, p. 315. The bull was issued from the Council of Vienne in 1311.

11. See P. Fredericq, *Corpus documentum inquisitionis haereticae . . .* 1889, Ist vol., No. 249. Quoted by W. Fraenger, *The Millenium of Hieronymus Bosch*, 1952, p. 26.

12. The apocryphal saying recorded here may easily be taken to refer to a future state in incarnation, but it almost certainly is intended to refer to the *post mortem* experience.

13. As almost all we know of the heretical groups we have from Inquisitorial records (cf. note 11 above), even fairly objective appraisals of these sects are unwittingly prejudiced. For the Free Spirits and Adamites, see G. Leff (note 10 above), p. 308ff. For the Free Spirits see R. Allier, *Les Frères et Soeurs des Espirit Libre*, 1905.

14. It is indeed recognised that the doctrines of the Free Spirits were never entirely extinguished in some parts of the Netherlands, Germany and Bohemia, and were probably influential in forming the teachings of the Anabaptists in Germany in the early sixteenth century.

15. Little work has been done on true heretical art. One may note in passing R. Nelli *et al*, *Les Cathares*, c. 1960, p. 288ff. on the esoteric design of Monsegur, W. Fraenger, *The Millenium of Hieronymus Bosch*,

1952, and the unreliable C. A. W. Aymès, *The Pictorial Language of Hieronymus Bosch*, 1975.

16. See for example Fraenger, note 11 above.

17. The little known is well summed up in R. H. Wilenski, *Flemish Painters 1430–1830*, Vol. I (1960), p. 496.

18. For an entertaining account of the mediaeval conception of the elements, see C. S. Lewis, *The Discarded Image*, 1971, p. 92ff.

19. *Genesis*, II, 17.

20. *Genesis*, I, 27.

21. *Genesis*, II, 7.

22. See for example H. P. Blavatsky, *The Secret Doctrine*, II, 1888, p. 1ff.

23. Quoted in Fraenger, note 11 above, p. 26–27.

24. See for example the tentative proposal in S. Runciman, *The Mediaeval Manichee*, 1969, p. 197.

25. The rulership of this *negative* Mars persisted until this present century, when the newly discovered Pluto was accorded rule over Scorpio. The planet was discovered in 1930, but at least one astrologer, calling it by name, accorded it rule over Scorpio as early as 1911: I. M. Pagan, *From Pioneer to Poet*, 1911, p. 103.

26. For a modern expression of this ancient idea, followed in a fairly materialistic vein by Lavatar, see for example K. Konig, 'The Zodiac' in *The Modern Mystic*, Feb. 1937, p. 12–14, and March 1937, p. 68–71.

27. See E. Panofsky, *Albrecht Durer*, 1945, Vol. I, p. 85: Panofsky traces the idea back to William of Conges [see Migne, *Pat. Lat.* 172, col. 55].

28. For the symbolism of the cock, see Guy de Tervarent, *Attributs et Symboles dans l'art Profane, 1450–1600. Dictionnaire d'un langage perdu*, 1958, p. 112ff & 248.

29. See for example, G. Leff (note 10 above), p. 308ff.

30. P. de Guevara, *Commentarios de la Pintura*, 1788.

31. M. van Vaernewijck, quoted by M. J. Friedlander, *Hieronymus Bosch*, 1941.

32. G. P. Lomazzo, *Tratto dell'Arte della Pittura, Scultura et Architettura*, 1584.

33. Fraenger, note 11 above.

34. Fray J. de Siguenza, *Historia de la Ordra de San Geronimo*, 1599.

35. See J. Combe, the article on *Bosch* in the McGraw-Hill *Encyclopedia of World Art*, 1960.

36. C. A. W. Aymes, *The Pictorial Language of Hieronymus Bosch*, English Edition, 1975.

37. A. Spychalska-Boczkowska, 'Material for the Iconography of Hieronymus Bosch's Triptych *The Garden of Delights*' in *Studia Muzealne*, 1966, p. 59.

38. C. de Tolnay, *Hieronymus Bosch*, 1937.

39. D. Bax, *Outcijfering van Jeroen Bosh*, 1949, quoted in W. Hirsch, *Hieronymus Bosch. The Garden of Delights*, 1954, p. 34.

40. M. J. Friedlander, see note 31 above.

41. The best English translation is the Caxton: *The Golden Legend or Lives of the Saints as Englished by William Caxton*, Vol. II, p. 225.

42. M. J. Friedlander, note 31 above, p. 7–8.

43. J. P. Lundy, *Monumental Christianity or the Art and Symbolism of the Primitive Church*, 1882, p. 133.

44. As G. Massey, that remarkable nineteenth century historian who influenced Blavatsky, put it, 'In the Hermean Zodiac, Pisces is named Ichton, and the fish is the female goddess who brought forth the young Sun-god as her fish'. *Natural Genesis*, p. 452.

45. A. Kircher, *Oedipus Aegyptiacus*, 1655.

46. W. Fraenger, see note 33 above.

47. Spychalska-Boczkowska, note 37 above, p. 59.

48. See for example Luc Gauricus, *Calendarium ecclesiasticum novum . . . 1552*, which lists a number of different versions of the so-called *Thema Mundi*. In the most ancient horoscope, traced back to the legendary Petosiris and Necepso (sic) the Moon and Ascendant are in 15 degrees of Cancer (see f. 8v). A second *thema* is given according to the Arabs and Egyptians (f.9r) which relates to the earlier one in listing the planets in their 'proper' signs, with the exception of the Sun (*Omnes planetae sunt in propriis domiciliis, preter Solem, qui erat in Libra Veneris domicilio*), since the theory behind this figure is that the world was created in the Autumn. It must be noted, however, that this latter figure gives a printer's error which places Saturn in Libra, when it is clearly intended, from the zodiacal order, that it should be in its own Capricorn, *domicilio Saturnis*.

49. Saint Ambrosius *De Paradiso*, 3, 13 p. 272 vol. XXXII *Corpus Scriptorum Ecclesiasticorum Latinorum*.

50. See for example G. Ferguson, *Signs and Symbols in Christian Art*, 1954, p. 27.

51. The examples given in figure 115 are from *Liber de magna Alchymia* a 16th century manuscript in the University Library, Leiden (Cod. Voss. Chym. Q.51). A sigil precisely the same in form as that painted by Bosch may be found in the 16th century alchemical collection in the Manuscript Department of the British Museum (Sl.830).

52. For a brief history of the four temperaments, see J. Evans, *Taste and Temperament*, 1939, Ch. 1.

53. See for example the detailed study of the melancholic temperament in Art, made with specific reference to Durer, *Saturn and Melancholy*, by R. Klibansky, E. Panofsky, and F. Saxl, 1964.

54. J. Taisnier, *Opus Mathematicum Octo Libros complectens*, 1562, p. 450ff.

55. J. Taisnier, note 54 above, p. 469

56. Tommaso Rangoni was probably the one to commission this picture: his relationship with the *Origin* is discussed by E. Mandowsky, '*The Origin of the Milky Way* in the National Gallery', *Burlington Magazine*, 1938, I, p. 88.

57. The only Italian edition I have had access to is the 1542 Venetian *Geoponica: Constantino cesare de li scelti et utilissimi documenti de l'Agricoltum, nuouvamente da latino in volgare tradotto per M. Nicolo Vitelli. . .* The story of the Milky Way is given in lib. XI, cap. xx, *Historia del Giglio*, p. 130v of this edition.

58. See Mandowsky, note 56 above.

59. Although the 'Copernican doctrine' was announced as a 'hypothesis' whilst Copernicus was professor in Rome, as early as 1500, the *De Revolutionibus* was not published until 1543, the year of his death. The new imagery associated with the heliocentric system did not begin to enter the non-specialist market until the seventeenth century.

THE DIVINE PRINCIPLES

1. W. Blake, *A Descriptive Catalogue of pictures, poetical and historical inventions, painted by William Blake . . .*, 1809.

2. Recorded as though verbatim by A. Cunningham, *The Lives of the Most Eminent British Painters and Sculptors*, 1844, Vol. II p. 158.

3. Perhaps one of the earliest suggestions that Blake had direct access to the spiritual world is in the analysis of Blake's horoscope in *Urania*, see note 26 below.

4. Until comparatively recently it was believed that Blake's parents were Swedenborgians: see D. Erdina, *Comparative Literature*, Eugene, University of Oregon, Vol. V, 1953.

5. S. F. Damon, *A Blake Dictionary*, 1965: 'Behmen's writings affected Blake profoundly, a fact generally overlooked, because Behmen is hard reading'. p. 40.

6. C. A. Muses, *Illumination on Jacob Boehme. The Works of Dionysius Freher*, 1951, p. 137.

7. See Damon, note 5 above, p. 7.

8. Material for Varley's life is taken from A. T. Story, *James Holmes and John Varley*, 1894, and from Cunningham, note 2 above.

9. Those who have chosen the word *geomancy* to denote their study of ley-lines and telluric currents have made a fundamental mistake: the word was already used in occult circles to denote the art of fortune telling by means of (originally) earth, by means of cast pebbles or stones, by means of marks made in the earth, and (latterly) by means of marks made on paper. The mistake in confusing this *mantia* with the ley-lines appears to have arisen with careless sin-ologists, who, searching for a European equivalent for the Chinese *Feng Shui*, an occult art distantly related to the ley-line studies, chose the word *geomancy*, presumably being ignorant of its precise meaning, but attracted by its Greek etymology. See my forthcoming *Dictionary of Occult, Hermetic and Alchemical Sigils*, Routledge and Kegan Paul, 1979.

10. The art of fortune telling by shades of the dead is frequently wrongly termed *necromancy*, which is in fact fortune telling by means of dead bodies, or by means of the illegitimate invasion of dead bodies by normally disincarnate spirits.

11. A. Cunningham, note 2 above, p. 167.

12. In J. Varley, *A Treatise on Zodiacal Physiognomy*, 1828.

13. A. Cunningham, note 2 above, p. 169.

14. See M. Butlin, *The Blake-Varley Sketchbook of 1819 in the Collection of M. D. E. Clayton-Stamm*, 1969.

15. See Varley, note 12 above. Blake made no mention of Gemini. Varley writes: 'With respect to the vision of the ghost of the Flea, seen by Blake, it agrees in countenance with one class of people under Gemini, which sign is the significator of the Flea . . . the neatness, elasticity, the tenseness of the Flea, are significant of the elegant dancing and fencing sign Gemini'.

16. P. E. Tomory, *The life and art of Henry Fuseli*, 1972.

17. Butlin, note 14 above, p. 29.

18. For an account of such beings see C. W. Leadbeater, *The Astral Plane*, 1933, p.44ff.

19. A. J. Davis, *The Diakka, and their earthly victims . . . being an explanation of much that is false and repulsive in spiritualism*, 1873.

20. A. Gilchrist, *Life of W. Blake, 'Pictor Ignotus'*, 1863.

21. There is no sign that Blake actually practised astrology himself: this is perhaps explicable in terms of Boehmian philosophy, for the German insists that whilst there is nothing wrong with astrology as a practical science, it deals only with the 'Outworld', and is not properly speaking the concern of the spiritual man—see *The Three Principles*, 34. 12.

22. For the extent of astrology at this time, see especially K. Thomas, *Religion and the Decline of Magic*, 1971.

23. E. Sibly, *A New and Complete Illustration of the Occult Sciences, or the Art of foretelling future events and contigencies, by the aspects, position, and influences, of the heavenly bodies*, 1790.

24. A. T. Story, *James Holmes and John Varley*, 1894, p. 246.

25. Story, note 24 above, p. 247.

26. The horoscope was published in diagram form, in the magazine *Urania: or, the Astrologer's Chronicle, and Mystical Magazine*, 1825.

27. For example, on one of the pages of the Varley-Blake sketchbook (see note 14 above), there are some sketch variants of designs linked with the zodiacal sign Virgo ♍ which, according to William Bell Scott, the last owner of the sketchbook before its loss, Varley saw as the 'foot of a maiden peering from under her skirt'. In fact the graphic etymology for this sigil has nothing to do with feet, or even with young maidens, but the tentative sketches reveal Varley's interest (see note 14, p. 31).

28. W. Law, *The Works of Jacob Behmen the Teutonic Theosopher*, 1764.

29. See in particular C. A. Muses, *The Works of Dionysius Freher*, 1951, which contains an excellent account of Boehme's view of the nature of Evil.

30. J. Boehme, *The Three Principles of the Divine Essence of the Eternal Dark, Light, and Temporary World*, in Law, note 28 above. Superficially, of course, the painting by Blake (figure 148) may be taken as an illustration from *Genesis* IV: however, there is no indication in the Bible that Adam and Eve even saw the body of Abel; nor is there any mention of the body at all. The Lord asked Cain what he had done because 'the voice of his brother's blood cried up to Him from earth'. Blake shows Adam and Eve as witnesses, and not God—yet this departure from the biblical text is an important element within the inner structural meaning of the painting.

31. *Three Principles*, note 30 above, xxi 12.

32. *Three Principles*, note 30 above, xxi 23.

33. See plates bound into the edition given under Law, note 28 above.

34. The word 'quality' in its Boehmian sense is frequently mistranslated and misunderstood: Boehme does not derive the word from the latin *qualitas*, but from the German *quellen*—it should therefore be translated as 'outpouring', which is precisely how it is *pictured* by Freher in figure 147.

35. In the alchemical tradition the pact between the four elements is denoted by the interaction of two triangles, representing the four elements: ✡ See my *Dictionary of Occult, Hermetic and Alchemical Sigils* to be published by Routledge and Kegan Paul, 1979; see also Damon, note 5 above, p. 40. The alchemical implications of this chain of symbolism is discussed in relation to the *Aurea Catena Homeri*, by R. D. Gray, *Goethe the Alchemist, A Study of Alchemical Symbolism in Goethe's Literary and Scientific*, 1952. The four elements of the *Outworld* is secured within the occult tradition, yet is peculiar in detail to both Boehme and Blake. The Fire element (*schrack* to Boehme, the *Luvah* of Blake); the Air (the *Light of Wisdom* to Boehme, the *Urizen* of Blake), the Water (the *schall* or Sound of Boehme, the *Tharmas* of Blake) and Earth (*Figure* or *Form*, reminding one of *Urthona* and of Blake's dictum 'that call'd Body is a portion of the soul discern'd by the five senses') are synonymous.

36. Boehme had a profound knowledge of the workings of the planets on the material plane (but see note 29 above). The fact is that Boehme's contribution to the study of esoteric symbolism has just not been fully appreciated. His famous 'seven properties', his *wirkende Eigenschaften*, were intimately linked to the seven planets, to a point where his most able commentator, Dionysius Freher, employed the conventional sigils for the planets to represent the workings of the principles (see British Museum mss. Add. 5789, *Paradox, emblemata, aenigmata, hieroglyphica . . .*). Indeed, as Muses (see note 6 above, p. 134) has pointed out, for Boehme, 'The celestial bodies of our solar system were merely the most obvious demonstration of the manifestation in the physical world of the different properties'. In *De Signatura Rerum*, 9:8, Boehme says 'There is not anything in the Being of all beings, but it has the seven properties in it'.

37. This personal occultism corresponds to Blake's view of the Three Worlds—Heaven and Hell, which exist simultaneously in God as the Opposition of Contraries—and the projection or outbirth of the Outer World of Nature.

38. Agrippa, *De Occulta Philosophia*, Lib. II, Cap. LII.

39. See for example G. W. Digby, *Symbol and Image in William Blake*, 1957, p. 94ff.

40. *Three Principles*, note 30 above, XXI 5.

41. See Duncan Sloss and J. P. R. Wallis, *The Prophetic Writings of William Blake*, 1926, 1.560. There is an ideological relationship between Blake's imaginative list (see Damon, note 5 above, p. 266) and the points raised by Jerome (see note 35 on page 168). One wonders indeed if Blake was familiar with the two Jesus children in concept, for in the face of the Seth-genealogy with which he is familiar, and which Boehme emphasises, he describes a second line from this *Caina* (see *Jerusalem* 62: 8–13), including the 'immoral women' given by Jerome.

42. Damon (note 5 above, p. 266) gives this 'heresy' as 'seventeenth century Jewish'—it is of course older even than Jerome, but it is probably the tradition given by Damon which influenced Blake.

43. J. Boehme, *Mysterium* 22.

COLOURED FIRE

1. The quotations in this paragraph are from L. J. F. Wijsenbeek, *Piet Mondrian*, 1968.

2. See M. Seuphor, *Piet Mondrian, sa vie, son oeuvre*, 1956 (English translation, 1957, p. 57).

3. See C. Bouleau, *The Painter's Secret Geometry. A Study of Composition in Art* (English edition), 1963, p. 248.

4. M. Seuphor, quoted by Bouleau, note 3, p. 249.

5. For a treatment of the Golden Section, see Bouleau, note 3 above, and M. Ghyka, *Le Numero d'or*, 1931.

6. H. P. Blavatsky, *Isis Unveiled: a master-key to the mysteries of ancient and modern science and theology*, 1877, and *The Secret Doctrine*, 1888. These titles were courageous attempts to provide an authentic record of occult traditions, which were almost diametrically opposed to the popular scientific thought of the late nineteenth century. The complex anthropogenesis described by Blavatsky was opposed to the loosely assimilated Darwinism of the time, for whilst it by no means separated the human strain from those of plants and animals, it postulated a greater antiquity for man than either of these forms, which were regarded as materialised deposits left over from human evolution. The real point of conflict, however, was that Theosophy related the evolution of man—and indeed the growth and collapse of his

civilisations—to the working of a spiritual world invisible to ordinary perception. *The Secret Doctrine*, which is written in a confused, learned, rambling and amusing—sometimes even brilliant—style, presents the first consistent syncretic occultism designed for modern European man.

7. The written works of N. H. J. Schoenmaekers which appears to have most profoundly influenced Mondrian are *Het Nieuwe Wereldbeeld*, 1915 and *Beginselen der Beeldende Wiskunde*, 1916.

8. Steiner's relationship with the Theosophical Movement is a curious one, and has been largely misunderstood. The historical facts are discussed briefly in Steiner, *The Course of My Life*, 1951 edition, Chapters 32 to 34, and the important difference between Theosophy and Anthroposophy is set out in the seminal work by R. Steiner, *The Occult Movement in the Nineteenth Century and its Relation to Modern Culture*, based on ten lectures given in Dornach, 1915. J. Ransom, *A Short History of The Theosophical Society*, 1936 glosses over the differences (see p. 397ff.) For Kandinsky's relationship with Steiner, see Ringbom, note 15 below.

9. W. Kandinsky, *Uber das Geistige in der Kunst*, 1912.

10. T. H. Robsjohn-Gibbings, *Mona Lisa's Moustache: A Dissection of Modern Art*, 1947.

11. See Robsjohn-Gibbings, note 10, p. 151–152.

12. Some accounts of the emergence of abstract art refer to the reaction of many artists to the emptiness of nineteenth-century academic art. However, though the best academic art was never empty, a healthy reaction to its sterile aspects was endemic in most nineteenth century painting from the Impressionists onwards. There was nothing in such a 'reaction' which would in itself lead to non-objective art.

Another explanation claims that the development of photography had a liberating influence, and led the painter to neglect his 'duty' as a social recorder. This explanation is banal, for whilst such a view of the artist's role is questionable, the influence of photographic discoveries on artists of real merit were constructive rather than destructive: in effect the camera opened up the familiar world of experience for much stimulating research. The reaction to the 'exact description' of the camera has been consistently over-estimated by art historians (an exception being A. Scharf, *Art and Photography*, 1968), and there is no evidence that the influence of ordinary photography led to non-objective art.

Yet another popular 'explanation' points to the development which may theoretically be traced from the work of Van Gogh and Cezanne to modern abstraction, the colour freedom established by Van Gogh and Gauguin, leading to the *Fauves*, was carried over into the work of Kandinsky, Marc and Chagall. Linked to this important and influential colour trend was the impetus towards distortion and restructuring of the physical world, arising from the work of Cezanne, which blossomed in the cubism of Picasso and Braque. This is 'cause and effect' art

history: the trends towards colour freedom and restructuring were deeply rooted in the study and manipulation of the familiar world, and linked with the exploration of the artist's emotional world. Non-objective art was founded on principles which rejected completely the mere physical world as a place of exploration. Mondrian and Kandinsky, for instance, did not paint the visible world in their later works, whereas Van Gogh and Cezanne were notorious for sitting out of doors in all weathers, the Dutchman pursued by his own inner demon, the Frenchman by his wife. Van Gogh might well have had sunstroke, Kandinsky never.

13. P. O. Runge, *Schriften, Fragmente, Briefe*, (ed. E. Forsthoff) 1938.

14. Gustav Moreau, for example, wrote, 'I am dominated by one thing, an irresistible, burning attraction towards abstraction' (quoted by J. Pierre, in J. Paladilhe and J. Pierre, *Gustave Moreau*, 1972), yet he was content to express the immutable with conventional forms: he was of course striving for the 'ideal' rather than the 'abstract' in its modern sense.

15. Kandinsky, *Ruckblicke*: but see S. Ringbom, *The Sounding Cosmos. A Study in the Spiritualism of Kandinsky and the Genesis of Abstract Painting*, 1970, p. 32.

16. F. Marc, *Briefe, Augzeighnungen und Aphorismen*, 1920.

17. Among the numerous occult books in his library were Steiner's important *Theosophy*, and his practical handbook with the notoriously mistranslated English title *Knowledge of the Higher Worlds*. For a study of these sources, see Ringbom, note 15 above.

18. In the theosophical magazine *Lucifer*, as early as September, 1896.

19. C. W. Leadbeater, *The Astral Plane: its inhabitants and phenomena*, 1895, p. 6ff.

20. Leadbeater, note 19 above, p. 26.

21. E. Babbit, *The Principles of Light and Color*, 1878, p. 446–447.

22. A. H. Nethercot, *The Last Four Lives of Annie Besant*, 1963, p. 50–53.

23. C. W. Leadbeater and A. Besant, *Thought-Forms*, 1905, p. 16ff. The quotations are from Nethercot, note 22 above.

24. Varley was more than a proficient water-colourist, specializing in oriental and Middle-eastern subjects; he was an astrologer, a Freemason, and a traveller (which no doubt accounted for his fluency in Arabic, Japanese, Spanish, Turkish, Greek, Italian and French). He has achieved the most curious fame of being the earliest subject of Leadbeater's clairvoyant experiments in the reading of past incarnations—he is indeed the *Erato* of the clairvoyant's reincarnation study, *The Soul's Growth Through Reincarnation. The Lives of Erato and Spica*, 1941 which gives a biography of the latest incarnation. Varley was born in 1850, and whilst the official reference books invariably give

his date of death as 1899, he was working with Besant in the new Adya building in India as late as 1907. A short obituary in *Art News* says he died in Cheltenham, 1933. His wife, Isabella Pollexfen, was the aunt of W. B. Yeats.

25. S. Ringbom, 'Art in "The Epoch of the Great Spiritual"—Occult Elements in the Early Theory of Abstract Painting', *The Journal of the Warburg Institute*, 29—1960.

26. Leadbeater and Besant, note 23 above, page 62.

27. Ringbom, note 15 above.

28. See Leadbeater and Besant, note 23 above. p. 75ff.

29. In view of Ringbom's excellent study on this picture (note 15 above), I have not delved deeply into the influence of either the theosophical teachings or of Steiner's teachings on the various elements within this composition, but have restricted myself to occult influences.

30. For a summary of the theosophical view, see A. E. Powell, *The Etheric Double*, for a summary of the anthroposophical, see G. Wachsmuth, *Etheric Formative Forces*, 1932.

31. A. Marques, *The Human Aura*, 1896?

32. A description with which Kandinsky would have been familiar is found in C. W. Leadbeater, *The Inner Life*, 1910, but the chakras were known and described in occult circles long before this time: in fact Leadbeater showed much misunderstanding of their nature, as Woodroffe insisted (see A. Avalon, *The Serpent Power, being the Shat-Chakra-Nirupana and Paduka-Panchaka*, 1924—especially the Introduction, which is critical of Leadbeater).

33. The plate reproduced in figure 169 is a hand-coloured engraving from J. G. Gichtel and J. G. Graber, *Eine kurze Eroffnung und Anweisung der dreyen Principien und Welten im Menschen*, 1799. Kandinsky probably did not know this plate, but would have been familiar with a reproduction given by Leadbeater in *The Chakras*, which was from a lithographic copy given in *Theosophica Practica*, 1897, a book which has been confused with one by Gichtel of the same title.

34. For a summary of the theosophical view of the Mental Body, see A. E. Powell, *The Mental Body*, 1927. This higher principle is called the Mental Body, though its actual connotation lifts it well out of the ordinary concept of *mentality*, into a much higher spiritual level, quite inaccessible to plants and animals.

35. It is interesting that the colours of this lower part of the composition into which these legs are inserted, symbolize according to the colour chart given by Leadbeater and Besant (note 23 above) 'selfishness', 'sensuality', 'depression', and 'fear'—in a word, all low-level human emotions. The darkness and turgidity of this low-grade stratification acts as the base for the simple triangular form of the composition. Kandinsky, in his *Concerning the Spiritual in Art* develops the spiritual nature, and compositional

value, of the triangle.

36. The order is related to the older theosophical planetary views—see for example that of Boehme, elucidated by C. A. Muses, *The Works of Dionysius Freher*, 1951, p. 130ff.

37. According to Leadbeater and Besant (note 23 above) these depict malice and affection. It might usefully be observed that these astral images are wrongly termed *thoughtforms*, for what makes them specific in shape and colour is not so much the thought as the sentience mingled with the thought. They might more accurately be termed 'emotive thought-forms'.

38. Leadbeater, note 19 above.

AS ABOVE, SO BELOW

1. J. Russell, *Max Ernst: life and work*, 1967.

2. Designed in 1941 for *View*, founded by C. H. Ford.

3. Collin de Plancy, *Dictionnaire Infernal*, probably the 1862 edition. The images were engraved by Jarrault after drawings by M. L. Breton, and one wonders if Ernst was playing with the namesake of his friend André Breton in choice of this artist.

4. See Plancy, note 3 above, and G. Davidson, *A Dictionary of Angels including the Fallen Angels*, 1967, and M. Psellus, *Dialogue between Timothy and Thracian, on the Operation of Daemons*.

5. See Psellus, note 4 above.

6. M. Ernst, from *An informal life of M.E.*, translated for example in *Max Ernst*, a catalogue to an Exhibition arranged by the Arts Council of Great Britain, 1961, and in *Some Data on the Youth of M.E.*, in *Max Ernst: Beyond Painting, and other Writings by Artists and Friends*, edited by R. Motherwell, 1948.

7. G. Bazin, *Histoire de l'avant-garde en peinture du XIIIe au XXe siecle*, 1969.

8. S. Dali, *Le Surrealism au Service de la Revolution, No. 1*, quoted in Motherwell, note 6 above.

9. The title is taken from the beginning of the original dedication to Breton: *Les Hommes n'en sauron rien*.

10. Russell, note 1 above.

11. G. de Chirico 'The Eternal Signs', in *On Metaphysical Art*, in *Metaphysical Art* by M. Carro, 1971.

12. This dictum is found in the first statement of the so-called Emerald Tablet—see J. F. Ruska, *Tabula Smaragdina*, 1926. According to the hermetic tradition there were two images of God—the Cosmos and man: see for example, G. R. S. Mead, *Thrice-Greatest Hermes. Studies in Hellenistic Theosophy and Gnosis*, 1964 ed., Vol. 3, p. 151. A modern interpretation of the macrocosm-microcosm relationship is R. Collin, *The Theory of Celestial Influences*, 1954.

13. My own translation.

14. Chirico, see note 18 below.

15. The profound influence was Ducasse's *Chants de Malador*. See for example the McGraw Hill Encyclopaedia of World Art, Vol. V, p. 217.

CREDITS

16. M. Ernst, *La Femme 100 Têtes. Avis au lecteur par André Breton*, 1929.

17. E. D. Babbit, *The Principles of Light and Color*, 1878.

18. Gorgio de Chirico, 'Metaphysical Aesthetics', in *Metaphysical Art*, by M. Carro, 1971.

19. The dualism which runs through occultism is derived ultimately from zoroastrianism: the principle of darkness is linked with the moon, and with *Ahriman*, the principle of light is linked with the sun, and with *Ahurah Mazdao*. See for example, R. Steiner, *Lucifer and Ahriman*, English translation, 1954.

20. See C. S. Lewis, *The Discarded Image*, 1964, chapter 5.

21. The artist herself emphasises the morality implicit within this imagery, commenting upon the Zoharistic teaching that if a man is away from his wife he should attach the Shekinha to himself 'in order that the perfection of union between male and female should not be unbalanced or disturbed'. It is because this evil man in the picture has not preserved this harmony that he is a prey to Lilith. (Letter to the author, dated March 18th, 1976).

22. See *The Talmud, Shabbath*, 151b and *'Erubin*, 100b. The exoteric legend that Lilith was Adam's first wife is found in Buxtorf's massive *Lexicon Chaldaicum Talmudicum*, 1630. According to the *Talmud, 'Erubin* 18b, Adam begot the demons after the expulsion from Eden, and within such a chronology Lilith would have been his second wife. Esoterically, however, Lilith appears to have been part of the curious Man-Woman created by God, according to *Genesis* I, 27, long before the creation of Adam.

23. E. A. W. Budge, *Amulets and Talismans*, 1961, p. 135.

24. G. Massey, *The Natural Genesis*, 1883, Vol. I, p. 450. For the later development into the *Chi-Ro*, see P. E. Testa, *Il Simbolismo dei Giudeo-Cristiani*, 1962.

25. A. Ehrenzweig, *The Hidden Order of Art*, 1967.

26. See *Shabbath* and *'Erubin*, note 22 above.

27. See T. Burckhardt, *Sacred Art in East and West*, 1967.

28. There is no reliable book dealing with the *trulli* symbols—not all of which are occult—but see M. L. T. Verardi, *I Misteriosi Simboli dei Trulli*, 1972.

29. The situation in regard to art reminds one of that in regard to esotericism in earlier times. See for example the famous letter from Trithemius dated 8th April, 1510 in H. C. Agrippa, *De Occulta Philosophia*, 1531. His words are worth repeating: Unum hoc tamen te monemus custodire preceptum, ut vulgaria vulgaribus, altiora vero et arcana altioribus atque secretis tantum communices amicis. Ad foenum bovi, saccarum psitaco tantum: intellige mentem, non bovum calcibus, ut plerisque; contigit subiiciaris. (None the less I advise you to observe one rule in this matter: that you pass on your vulgar secrets to the vulgar and your elevated and secret truths to elevated and secret friends. Give hay to an ox, sugar to a parrot. Understand the sense of what I say, lest as often happens, you should happen to be trod beneath the feet of the oxen).

I would like to thank Steve Adamson for his preliminary reading of the draft text, and for his sensitive and constructive advice as both editor and friend; and I would like also to thank Prue Chennells for doing the final editing with such love and care. It goes almost without saying that I am indebted for help given by the staffs of numerous libraries, museums and galleries: I must thank especially those who made facilities available to me in the Bodleian, Oxford; the Institute of Historical Research, London; the National Galleries in Copenhagen, London, Madrid, and the Louvre, Paris; the National Libraries in Florence, London and Paris; the Public Libraries in Leeds and Lucca; the Library in the Society for Psychical Research, London; the Mauritshuis in The Hague; the Tate Gallery, London, and the Uffizi, Florence; the University Libraries in Bari, Leiden, the Sorbonne, Sussex, and University College, London, and the Library of the Warburg Institute, London. The photographs were taken or provided as follows: Bayerische Staatsbibliothek, Munich, 85; Boymans, Rotterdam, 161, 166; British Museum, 5, 7, 10, 11, 12, 19, 21, 23, 38, 54, 61, 125; Elio Ciol, 41; John Freeman, 79, 80; Guggenheim Museum, New York, 166; Haags Gemeentemuseum, 178; National Gallery, London, 35, 64, 68, 77, 84, 91, 116, 123, 128, 133; National Museum, Copenhagen, 32, 39, 40, 50, 66; National Museum, Nuremberg, 36; the Prado, 9, 112, 113, 121, 122; Tate Gallery, 139, 140, 144, 153, 167, 168, 188, 192, 200; Jeff Teasdale, 179; Uffizi, 6, 70; Victoria and Albert Museum, 37, 130, 141; John Webb, 148. The remaining photographs were taken by the author.

INDEX